PRIDE AND PREJUDICE

JANE AUSTEN

NOTES BY PAUL PASCOE

 Longman

The right of Paul Pascoe to be identified as Author of this Work
has been asserted by him in accordance with the
Copyright, Designs and Patents Act 1988

YORK PRESS
322 Old Brompton Road, London SW5 9JH

PEARSON EDUCATION LIMIT ED
Edinburgh Gate, Harlow,
Essex CM20 2JE, United Kingdom
Associated companies, branches and representatives throughout the world

First published 1998
This new and fully revised edition first published 2002
Ninth impression 2008

ISBN: 978-0-582-50620-6

Designed by Michelle Cannatella
Illustrated by Susan Scott
Typeset by Land & Unwin (Data Sciences), Bugbrooke, Northamptonshire
Produced by Pearson Education Asia Limited, Hong Kong

CONTENTS

PREFACE

York Notes are designed to give you a broader perspective on works of literature studied at GCSE and equivalent levels. With examination requirements changing in the twenty-first century, we have made a number of significant changes to this new series. We continue to help students to reach their own interpretations of the text but York Notes now have important extra-value new features.

You will discover that York Notes are genuinely interactive. The new **Checkpoint** features make sure that you can test your knowledge and broaden your understanding. You will also be directed to excellent websites, books and films where you can follow up ideas for yourself.

The **Resources** section has been updated and an entirely new section has been devoted to how to improve your grade. Careful reading and application of the principles laid out in the Resources section guarantee improved performance.

The **Detailed summaries** include an easy-to-follow skeleton structure of the story-line, while the section on **Language and style** has been extended to offer an in-depth discussion of the writer's techniques.

The Contents page shows the structure of this study guide. However, there is no need to read from the beginning to the end as you would with a novel, play or poem. Use the Notes in the way that suits you. Our aim is to help you with your understanding of the work, not to dictate how you should learn.

Our authors are practising English teachers and examiners who have used their experience to offer a whole range of **Examiner's secrets** – useful hints to encourage exam success.

The General Editor of this series is John Polley, Senior GCSE Examiner and former Head of English at Harrow Way Community School, Andover.

The author of these Notes is Paul Pascoe, who has been a Chief and Principal Examiner in English since 1974. Author of a number of textbooks for Secondary pupils, he was until recently Head of English at Formby High Comprehensive School.

The edition used in these Notes is the Penguin Classics Edition, 1996, edited with an introduction and notes by Vivien Jones.

PART ONE

INTRODUCTION

HOW TO STUDY A NOVEL

A novelist starts with a story that examines a situation and the actions of particular characters. Remember that authors are not photographers, and that a novel never resembles real life exactly. Ultimately, a novel represents a view of the world that has been created in the author's imagination.

There are six features of a novel:

❶ THE STORY: this is the series of events, deliberately organised by the writer to test the characters

❷ THE CHARACTERS: the people who have to respond to the events of the story. Since they are human, they can be good or bad, clever or stupid, likeable or detestable, etc. They may change too!

❸ THE VIEWPOINT/VOICE: who is telling the story. The viewpoint may come from one of the characters, or from an omniscient (all-seeing) narrator, which allows the novelist to write about the perspectives of all the characters

❹ THE THEMES: these are the underlying messages, or meanings, of the novel

❺ THE SETTING: this concerns the time and place that the author has chosen for the story

❻ THE LANGUAGE AND STYLE: these are the words that the author has used to influence our understanding of the novel

To arrive at the fullest understanding of a novel, you need to read it several times. In this way, you can see how all the choices the author has made add up to a particular view of life, and develop your own ideas about it.

The purpose of these York Notes is to help you understand what the novel is about and to enable you to make your own interpretation. Do not expect the study of a novel to be neat and easy: novels are chosen for examination purposes, not written for them!

EXAMINER'S SECRET

When using a quotation, write it *exactly* as it appears in the novel.

AUTHOR – LIFE AND WORKS	CONTEXT
1775 Born 16 December daughter of Rev. George Austen, the seventh child of eight	**1775** American War of Independence begins
	1780 Gordon Riots
	1783 Britain recognises independence of USA
1787–9 Earliest writings including *A History of England*	**1788** Parliamentary motion to abolish Slave Trade
	1789 French Revolution begins
1795–8 Original versions of *Northanger Abbey, Sense and Sensibility* and *Pride and Prejudice*	**1792** Mary Wollstencroft publishes *A Vindication of the Rights of Women*
	1793 France declares war on Britain, Holland and Spain
1801 Father retires; family moves to Bath	**1798** Nelson defeats French fleet
1805 Father dies	**1801** Act of Union of Britain and Ireland comes into force
1806 Moves to Southampton with mother and sister, Cassandra	**1805** Nelson defeats Franco-Spanish fleet at Trafalgar
1809 Moves to village of Chawton in Hampshire	**1808** Duke of Wellington defeats French at Vimiero
1811 *Sense and Sensibility* published	**1811** Because of king's insanity Prince of Wales becomes Prince Regent; Luddites destroy machinery
1813 *Pride and Prejudice* published	
1814 *Mansfield Park* published	
1816 *Emma* published. Completes *Persuasion*	**1814** Stephenson's first practical steam locomotive
1817 Moves to Winchester for medical attention. Dies on 18 July. Buried in Winchester Cathedral on 29 July	**1815** Napoleon defeated at Waterloo
1818 *Northanger Abbey* and *Persuasion* published jointly with preface by her brother Hartley	

SETTING AND BACKGROUND

CHECK THE BOOK

Jane Austen's Northanger Abbey is an amusing reminder that the author had a tongue-in-cheek attitude to the **romantic fiction** on which her plots are based.

Jane Austen's novels contain little description and few references to background details. Nevertheless, Jane Austen presents us with a fully imagined world.

SOCIAL STRUCTURES

Jane Austen would have partitioned society into aristocracy, gentry and common people.

Most of Jane Austen's characters are members of the gentry. They were largely a land-owning class, but included others, such as Anglican clergy. Tradespeople were excluded. There were also divisions within the gentry. Fitzwilliam Darcy, in contrast to Mr Bennet, comes from an ancient family and, although not titled, commands a status above that of many of the nobility, such as Lady Catherine.

By the end of the eighteenth century, however, the social fabric was already changing. In particular, the distinction between landed gentry and city tradespeople had become blurred. Darcy's 'rejection' of Lady Catherine and his intimacy with the Gardiners is a kind of symbolic reflection of these changes. Sir William Lucas is a tradesman but is determined to prove himself a member of the gentry.

MANNERS AND VALUES

The title 'gentleman' accorded one social privilege but it also assumed certain standards of behaviour. There were clear procedures regarding visiting, introductions, forms of address, social conversation, order of precedence and the formal relationships between the sexes. Raw emotions were never to be displayed openly in public.

The art of conversation performed an important social role. In theory, the outward formalities and civilities reflected inner values and moral standards. The reality, however, fell short of the ideal and Jane Austen constantly exposes the mismatch between the social and moral scales.

MARRIAGE AND WEALTH

Among the well-to-do at least, marriage was much more like a business transaction than it is today.

Even among lesser families, marriage contracts could include complex financial conditions. However, by the end of the eighteenth century, young people exercised more freedom of choice; arranged marriages, such as that proposed by Lady Catherine, had already died out by Jane Austen's day.

 DID YOU KNOW?

Marrying for money may seem unromantic but the so-called 'pre-nuptial' contracts among the very rich are a modern-day equivalent of earlier marriage contracts.

For women, marriage was often the only means of social improvement. Romance apart, Elizabeth is successful because she has secured upward mobility and security for herself and her family.

The question of money forms a foil to romance; Jane Austen was never less than a realist in this respect. It is difficult to draw absolute parallels with today's values, but Mr Bennet's £2,000 per annum or Darcy's £10,000 per annum needs to be seen in light of other typical incomes:

- A successful tradesman like Mr Gardiner might expect to earn £700 per annum (some, of course became very rich indeed)

- A shopkeeper might aspire to about £150 a year

- A tenant farmer might receive about £120

- An agricultural worker had to survive on about £30 a year

- To run Bingley's carriage alone, would have needed an income of between £800 to £1000 a year

SETTING

Longbourn will have comprised the house, a farm and associated houses. Mr Bennet will probably have employed an agent to run his estate.

Pemberley will have been a community in its own right with many dependent on it for their livelihood.

Social gatherings were particularly important in Jane Austen's day.

The ball, the musical evening and the card-table were at the centre of social life and could bring together a surprisingly diverse range of people. Communities such as Meryton would raise money by subscription to support public dances or 'assemblies'. The local inn was often the venue. There was an increasing trend, however, towards the staging of private balls at large country houses. Either way, such occasions were seen as an opportunity for matchmaking.

By the end of the nineteenth century, the better off were significantly more mobile. New 'turnpike' roads made it possible to travel easily from town to country. But transport was expensive; very few could maintain their own carriage. Mr Bennet's horses, for instance, are often needed for farm work. Except for the likes of Darcy and Bingley, a journey of any distance was an adventure.

HISTORICAL AND LITERARY BACKGROUND

Jane Austen's life coincided with a period of political upheaval. Revolutionary cries of personal liberty and freedom had swept through Europe and extended to the New World, precipitating the United States Declaration of Independence in 1776 and the French Revolution in 1789. For most of Jane Austen's adult life Britain was at war with France.

In the field of the arts, the **Romantic** movement, which stressed the importance of imagination and personal emotion, was approaching its height. The poets, Wordsworth and Coleridge, the painter, J.M.W. Turner, the composer, Beethoven and Jane Austen were all born within five years of one another.

However, there is barely a hint of these tumultuous times in Jane Austen's work. She preferred to scrutinise the emotional ripples within a comparatively settled and familiar society than to chart the tempestuous seas of distant revolution. Artistically, she drew her strength from the example of the great eighteenth-century prose writers, such as Dr Johnson, whose cool, well-ordered, witty and incisive observations on life formed the basis of her style. The passion of Romanticism did not inspire her. In fact, in her last novel, *Persuasion*, the heroine is found discouraging a lovelorn young man from reading the emotionally charged poetry of the day.

EXAMINER'S SECRET
You will gain more credit if you can show you have some understanding of the novel in its historical context.

She was, however, influenced by a band of mainly women writers of **romantic novels** with titles like *Belinda*, *The Old Manor House* and *Almeyda, Queen of Grenada*. Today, names such as Fanny Burney, Maria Edgeworth, Mrs Radcliffe, Charlotte Smith and Sophia Lee are perhaps familiar only to the specialist but they were immensely popular at the beginning of the nineteenth century. Jane Austen chose to build her plots along the lines of popular fiction but turned them sharply to her own ends (see **Structure**).

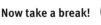 **Now take a break!**

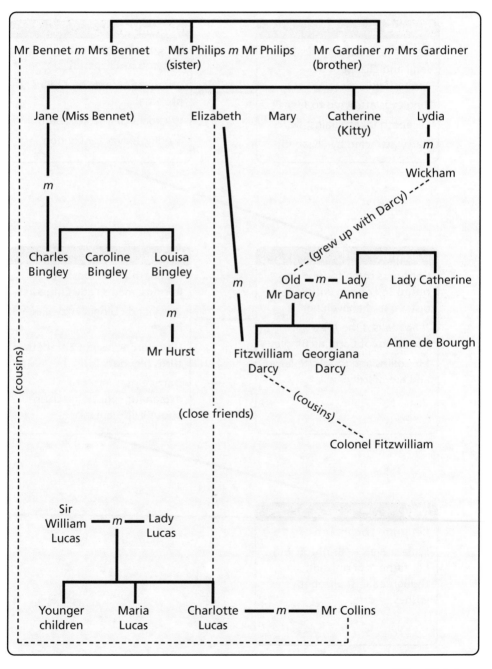

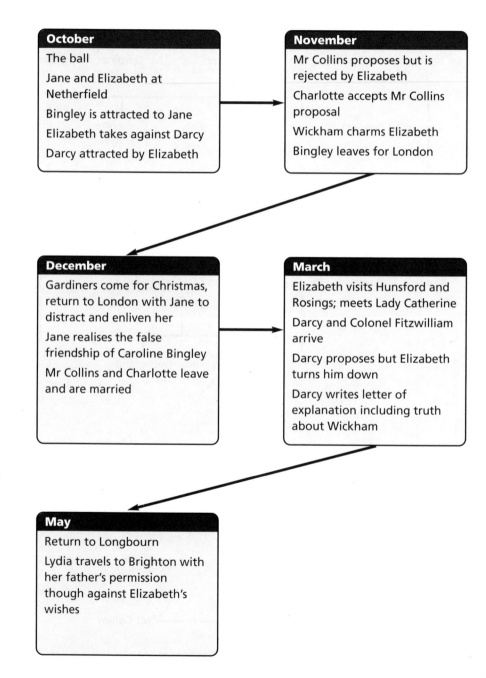

October

The ball

Jane and Elizabeth at Netherfield

Bingley is attracted to Jane

Elizabeth takes against Darcy

Darcy attracted by Elizabeth

November

Mr Collins proposes but is rejected by Elizabeth

Charlotte accepts Mr Collins proposal

Wickham charms Elizabeth

Bingley leaves for London

December

Gardiners come for Christmas, return to London with Jane to distract and enliven her

Jane realises the false friendship of Caroline Bingley

Mr Collins and Charlotte leave and are married

March

Elizabeth visits Hunsford and Rosings; meets Lady Catherine

Darcy and Colonel Fitzwilliam arrive

Darcy proposes but Elizabeth turns him down

Darcy writes letter of explanation including truth about Wickham

May

Return to Longbourn

Lydia travels to Brighton with her father's permission though against Elizabeth's wishes

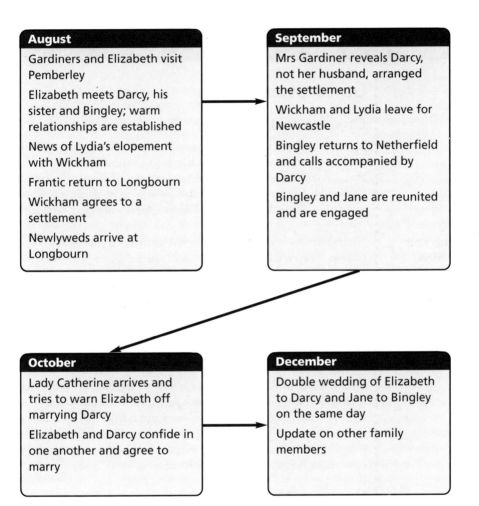

August

Gardiners and Elizabeth visit Pemberley

Elizabeth meets Darcy, his sister and Bingley; warm relationships are established

News of Lydia's elopement with Wickham

Frantic return to Longbourn

Wickham agrees to a settlement

Newlyweds arrive at Longbourn

September

Mrs Gardiner reveals Darcy, not her husband, arranged the settlement

Wickham and Lydia leave for Newcastle

Bingley returns to Netherfield and calls accompanied by Darcy

Bingley and Jane are reunited and are engaged

October

Lady Catherine arrives and tries to warn Elizabeth off marrying Darcy

Elizabeth and Darcy confide in one another and agree to marry

December

Double wedding of Elizabeth to Darcy and Jane to Bingley on the same day

Update on other family members

PART TWO

SUMMARIES

GENERAL SUMMARY

CHAPTERS 1–12

Mr and Mrs Bennet live at Longbourn in Hertfordshire, near to the small town of Meryton. Mrs Bennet, who is a very silly woman, is obsessed with finding husbands for her daughters. She is partly justified because Mr Bennet's estate is 'entailed' so that, on his death, it will pass to his cousin, Mr Collins, and his daughters will inherit nothing.

? DID YOU KNOW?
'Fitzwilliam' was the surname of Darcy's mother; it was quite common at the time to give a son his mother's maiden name as a forename.

Her prayers seem about to be answered when a rich young bachelor, Charles Bingley, takes up residence at Netherfield, bringing with him his two sisters and his wealthy friend, Fitzwilliam Darcy.

At the town ball, Bingley, who is liked by all, immediately falls in love with the eldest daughter, Jane, while Darcy is attracted to her vivacious sister, Elizabeth. Like most of the company, however, Elizabeth finds Darcy proud and disagreeable.

Elizabeth has further opportunities to observe the Bingleys and Darcy at close quarters when she stays with Jane at Netherfield. She has some animated conversations with Darcy that confirm her view that he is arrogant and intolerant. He, however, finds himself 'bewitched' (Ch. 10, p. 46) by her lively spirit. Elizabeth also doubts the sincerity of Caroline Bingley, whom she finds 'supercilious' (Ch. 6, p. 21).

CHAPTERS 13–23

Mr Bennet receives an extraordinary letter from his cousin, the Reverend Mr Collins, announcing his imminent arrival and hinting at his intention of marrying one of the sisters. He turns out to be an opinionated oaf who is constantly showing servile deference to Lady Catherine de Bourgh who had presented him with his living and who also happens to be Darcy's aunt. Meanwhile, there is another arrival in the district, George Wickham, a young officer in the Militia which has been garrisoned in Meryton. He quickly makes a favourable impression on Elizabeth who finds his company charming and entertaining. He claims that in the past Darcy has treated him most unjustly. Elizabeth is shocked by Wickham's story which serves to intensify her dislike of Darcy.

A ball is arranged at Netherfield but Wickham fails to appear. Elizabeth believes that Darcy is responsible for his absence and refuses to believe warnings that she should not accept Wickham at face value. Elizabeth's evening ends in misery when she has to witness members of her family behaving with embarrassing vulgarity.

Mr Collins duly proposes to Elizabeth and though hurt by her firm refusal quickly transfers his attentions to Elizabeth's closest friend, Charlotte Lucas, who immediately accepts his offer of marriage. Elizabeth is shocked, feeling that Charlotte has demeaned herself, but promises to visit her in Kent.

The Bingleys and Darcy suddenly decide to quit Netherfield for London. Elizabeth suspects that Bingley's sisters and Darcy want to separate him from Jane.

CHAPTERS 24–38

Jane is invited to London to stay with her aunt and uncle, the Gardiners. There are brief hopes that Jane will meet Bingley once again but Caroline Bingley's offhand treatment of Jane make it clear that she does not wish the acquaintance to be renewed. Jane is quietly heartbroken, whilst Elizabeth is depressed for her sister's sake.

Elizabeth fulfils her promise to visit Charlotte and is saddened that her friend seems quite satisfied by her comfortable but loveless existence. She is appalled by Lady Catherine's domineering and insolently arrogant manner, so much so that she actually welcomes the arrival of Darcy and his cousin. Darcy is so captivated by Elizabeth that he suddenly proposes to her, at the same time making it clear how he has had to put aside their differences in rank. Elizabeth is furious and refuses him on the grounds that his proud attitude is ungentlemanly, that he has deprived her sister of her happiness and that he had mistreated Wickham. The next day Darcy hands Elizabeth a long letter justifying his behaviour and exposing Wickham as a liar.

CHECK THE NET
There is no shortage of web sites devoted to Jane Austen and her novels. It's best to confine your search to specific information about a character, for example, or you may be overwhelmed.

GLOSSARY
supercilious snooty

Elizabeth is forced to acknowledge the truth of Darcy's explanation, including his remarks on her family's ill-breeding.

CHAPTERS 39–50

CHECK THE NET

Search for 'Chatsworth' or 'landscape gardens' to gain some impression of what Darcy's estate was like.

On returning to Longbourn, Elizabeth is ashamed that her father has permitted the flighty Lydia to follow the Militia to Brighton. She is relieved to escape with her aunt and uncle on a trip to Derbyshire. Believing the family to be away she agrees to visit Pemberley, Darcy's great estate. She is astonished to learn from the housekeeper how much Darcy is loved and respected by all the local people. Her astonishment is even greater when, returning unexpectedly, Darcy proves entirely affable and especially courteous towards her aunt and uncle.

Elizabeth begins to realise that she could love Darcy but her dreams are shattered when news arrives that Lydia has eloped with Wickham. On returning to Longbourn, the situation seems hopeless. Elizabeth doubts that Wickham has any intention of marrying Lydia and the visits of 'sympathetic' neighbours only serve to emphasise the disgrace and leave Elizabeth in despair. However, before long Mr Gardiner writes to say that he has come to an arrangement with Wickham and the couple are to be married. Mrs Bennet is ecstatic.

CHAPTERS 51–61

An unrepentant Lydia lets slip that Darcy was at the wedding. In response to Elizabeth's urgent enquiry about the truth of the matter, Mrs Gardiner explains that it was in fact Darcy who enforced the marriage. Overcome with gratitude and respect, Elizabeth dares to wonder whether Darcy did it for her.

Soon after Lydia and Wickham leave, Bingley and Darcy arrive. Bingley clearly still loves Jane but Darcy behaves stiffly and says very little. Before long, Bingley proposes to Jane and there is joy all round.

Lady Catherine makes a surprise visit and demands that Elizabeth should deny that she and Darcy are engaged. When he learns of Elizabeth's refusal, Darcy is encouraged to propose again. This time Elizabeth accepts.

DETAILED SUMMARIES

CHAPTERS 1–2 – Introducing the Bennets

1   Mrs Bennet is desperate to marry off her daughters.

2   She begs her husband to formally visit a Mr Bingley, a rich young bachelor, who has just moved into the neighbourhood.

3   She declares that she has five 'grown up' (Ch. 1, p. 6) daughters. We learn later that the youngest, Lydia, is just fifteen.

4   Mr Bennet infuriates his wife by apparently showing little interest but finally confesses that he has already visited Bingley.

The novel opens in the Bennet family home, which comprises the house and village of Longbourn, lying about a mile outside the small country town of Meryton. Mr and Mrs Bennet have five daughters and we are immediately made aware that Mrs Bennet's one concern in life is to see them married. She becomes increasingly frustrated and agitated at Mr Bennet's seeming indifference at the appearance in the neighbourhood of an eligible bachelor, Mr Bingley. Without Mr Bennet first paying a formal visit, the chance of making this vital acquaintance will be lost. For his part, Mr Bennet is content to tease his wife and express good-natured amusement at yet another demonstration of her 'nerves' (Ch. 1, p. 6).

In point of fact, Mr Bennet has fulfilled his obligations and already visited Mr Bingley but he extracts as much enjoyment as he can from keeping his family in ignorance. Mrs Bennet continues to sulk, despite Elizabeth's reassurances, until her despondency vanishes instantly on hearing the truth.

The opening chapter is the briefest in the novel and is almost entirely made up of conversation. Yet we are immediately drawn into the situation. We are presented with a first-hand encounter with Mrs Bennet's obsession with marriage and her 'mean understanding' (Ch. 1, p. 7). Likewise, we feel the force of Mr Bennet's 'sarcastic humour' (Ch. 1, p. 7). We also pick up some details of the family and friends.

> **CHECKPOINT 1**
>
> Think about the opening sentence. Is it true, even today? (There are all those magazines devoted to romance and marriage among the rich.) Is it poking fun? Is it serious? Is it a bit of both?

CHECK THE FILM

In the most recent BBC adaptation (1996), the famous opening sentence is given to Elizabeth rather than to a narrator. Why do you think it's handled this way?

Most importantly, we are left in no doubt of the importance of marriage, not only to Mrs Bennet but to society at large.

Establishing attitudes

The famous opening sentence introduces us to the main subject of the novel in an amusing and **ironic** way. The opening words, 'It is a truth universally acknowledged', sound like the introduction to some grand philosophical insight but the sentence goes on to deliver what seems like a ridiculous **anticlimax**. What of love, we may ask? What of the single man's feelings? The irony is that in reality, the statement is nearer to the mark than we might care to admit, even today!

CHAPTERS 3–5 – First impressions

1 After paying a brief courtesy visit on Mr Bennet, Mr Bingley leaves suddenly for London, only to return with a 'large party' (Ch. 3, p. 11) including his two sisters and his friend, Darcy.

2 At the local ball, Bingley is much admired but Darcy is felt to be too proud and he makes a bad impression on Elizabeth.

3 To Mrs Bennet's delight, Bingley seems very attracted to Jane.

4 We learn about Bingley's background, of his 'openness' and of his 'steady friendship' (Ch. 4, p. 16) with Darcy, who is 'clever' but 'haughty' and 'reserved' (Ch. 4, p. 17).

DID YOU KNOW?

Blue coats were very fashionable. They became all the rage in imitation of the main character of a romantic novel, *The Sorrows of Young Werther* by the German writer, Goethe (1774).

5 Elizabeth's friend, Charlotte Lucas, defends Darcy by arguing that with all his wealth he has a '*right* to be proud' (Ch. 5, p. 19).

Mr Bingley performs the customary courtesy of returning Mr Bennet's visit but the ladies are able to gain only a fleeting glimpse of his blue coat from an upstairs window. Mrs Bennet pictures one of her daughter's happily married in Netherfield, the country house that Bingley has rented, but her immediate plans of matchmaking are dashed by the news that Bingley has returned to London to bring down a 'large party for the ball' (Ch. 3, p. 11). In fact, he brings only five: his two sisters, his brother-in-law, Mr Hurst and a friend, Mr Darcy. The ball in question is one of the regular public 'assemblies', popular at the time, at which people could meet, converse, see and be seen. Consequently Bingley and his party come under close scrutiny. Bingley proves to be good-natured and outgoing. He rapidly gains everyone's approval but his friend, Darcy, handsome though he is, appears cold, distant and unfriendly.

DID YOU KNOW?
Mr Darcy is reputed to have an income of £10,000 a year which is probably about £350,000 in modern terms.

EXAMINER'S SECRET
There is no need always to provide lengthy quotations. Key words like 'steady', taken from the text can be more effective.

Indeed, Elizabeth overhears him expressing his thorough dislike of the occasion in general and poor impression of her in particular. Elizabeth laughs off the insult by relating the incident to her friends with great amusement but Mrs Bennet is able only to 'quite detest the man' (Ch. 3, p. 14). Otherwise, the ball is deemed a great success and Mrs Bennet returns home, joyful at the fact that Mr Bingley found Jane 'quite beautiful' (Ch. 3, p. 14) and actually danced with her twice.

We learn that Bingley and his sisters are extremely wealthy and that he may be seeking to purchase a country estate. We are also told of Bingley's dependence on his good friend Darcy's judgement and superior intelligence. The two men's characters are contrasted through their reactions to the ball. Bingley is delighted at the pleasant company and the exceptionally pretty girls, whereas Darcy finds the company dull and unfashionable although he grants that Miss Bennet (Jane) is tolerably pretty, despite smiling too much.

DID YOU KNOW?
In Jane Austen's day, the title 'Miss' was reserved for the eldest unmarried daughter in a family, so that Miss Bennet refers to Jane.

Chapters 3–5 continued

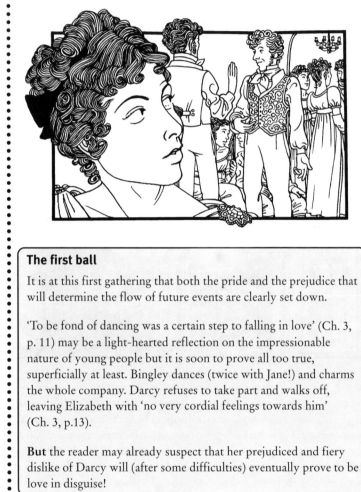

 DID YOU KNOW?

Elizabeth is known as 'Lizzy' by her family, 'Eliza' by friends and neighbours whilst the author refers to her as 'Elizabeth' in the narrative.

The first ball

It is at this first gathering that both the pride and the prejudice that will determine the flow of future events are clearly set down.

'To be fond of dancing was a certain step to falling in love' (Ch. 3, p. 11) may be a light-hearted reflection on the impressionable nature of young people but it is soon to prove all too true, superficially at least. Bingley dances (twice with Jane!) and charms the whole company. Darcy refuses to take part and walks off, leaving Elizabeth with 'no very cordial feelings towards him' (Ch. 3, p.13).

But the reader may already suspect that her prejudiced and fiery dislike of Darcy will (after some difficulties) eventually prove to be love in disguise!

The Bennets are visited by some of the children of their close friends, Sir William and Lady Lucas. Sir William is newly risen in the world having made a modest fortune in trade, but is very anxious to forget his background and prove himself a true country gentleman. Although he is uncommonly proud of his title, he and his wife are a naturally pleasant and friendly couple.

Charlotte Lucas is Elizabeth's closest friend whose views on love and marriage emerge, during the course of the novel, as very different from those of Elizabeth. Several opinions of Mr Darcy are offered. Mrs Bennet finds him thoroughly disagreeable and a 'horrid man' (Ch. 3, p. 14). Jane, who sees the best in everyone, suggests that he is naturally shy and reserved. Charlotte, however, feels that in view of his wealth and background, he has much to be proud about. Elizabeth admits that her pride has been hurt. The bookish Mary offers some thoughts on the distinction between pride and vanity, which everybody ignores.

CHECK THE BOOK

It may be constructive to compare the lively Elizabeth in *Pride and Prejudice* with the rather more smug Emma in *Emma* or the more reflective Anne in *Persuasion*.

Darcy's pride

Darcy's infamous pride emerges at the assembly. It colours Elizabeth's outlook until the truth begins to emerge in his letter (Chapters 35–6). Darcy later attributes his behaviour to shyness but his contempt for narrow country society is expressed elsewhere. At the same time, Darcy's manner sparks off an instinctive prejudice against one who is rich, powerful and can come and go as he pleases.

Darcy's cool aloofness is precisely what makes him fascinating.

Throughout the novel, Jane is presented as naively and unrealistically prejudiced in people's favour. However, her readiness to admit the possibility that Darcy is shy in strange company, shows her, on this occasion, to be more dispassionate than Elizabeth and less prone to jump to easy conclusions. How people are to be judged is a recurrent theme in the novel and at moments such as this, Jane Austen makes clear that no one has a monopoly of insight.

GLOSSARY
cordial warm, friendly

CHAPTER 6 – The ladies size each other up

1 The Bennet ladies and Bingley's sisters visit each other.

2 Everybody is polite but Elizabeth thinks the sisters are snobbish and 'supercilious' (p. 21), whilst Bingley's sisters detest Mrs Bennet.

3 Bingley is clearly drawn to Jane but Elizabeth and Charlotte Lucas disagree as to what Jane's reaction should be.

4 Darcy begins to take an interest in Elizabeth.

CHECKPOINT 2

How do Elizabeth's and Charlotte's views on marriage affect the decisions they take?

Acquaintances deepen as a result of an exchange of visits between Longbourn and Netherfield. Bingley's sisters are prepared to entertain an interest in Jane and Elizabeth but find Mrs Bennet 'intolerable' (p. 21) and wholly disregard the other sisters. For her part, Elizabeth continues to find their attitude patronising and feels that their apparent warmth is entirely owing to Bingley's feelings for Jane. Jane is clearly falling in love with Bingley but Elizabeth and Charlotte are divided as to how she should behave. Elizabeth feels that a relationship should develop naturally and that the man will soon recognise the woman's sincere feelings. Charlotte is more hard-headed and worldly, feeling that the woman should be more assertive lest the chance of a financially attractive marriage be lost. In any case, she argues, however well a couple know each other in courtship, whether they will be happy in marriage is 'a matter of chance' (p. 22). Unsuspecting the future turn of events, Elizabeth laughs that Charlotte herself would never act according to these principles.

Meanwhile, Darcy finds himself attracted to Elizabeth, less by her moderate beauty than by her liveliness and expressive dark eyes. Her particular charms are illustrated as she plays and sings to the company. She is less technically accomplished than her sister, Mary, but her performance is much more natural and pleasurable.

 DID YOU KNOW?

In Jane Austen's day it was not usually acceptable for a woman to decline an offer to dance.

Elizabeth is taken aback at Darcy's request to dance with her (all the more surprising, given his general distaste for the practice) and is 'determined' (p. 25) to decline the offer, believing him to be acting only out of formal politeness. To Miss Bingley's astonishment, Darcy confesses his interest in Elizabeth. She displays immediate signs of jealousy in her sarcastic jibe about the possibility of Mrs Bennet as mother-in-law.

CHAPTERS 7–9 – Men in uniform arrive!

❶ Mr Bennet's circumstances are explained; his estate is 'entailed' (Ch. 7, p. 27) to a distant relative.

❷ News of the arrival of a regiment in Meryton thrills the youngest daughters, Kitty and Lydia, not to mention Mrs Bennet.

❸ Jane is invited to dine with the Bingleys at Netherfield but catches a cold and is forced to stay; Elizabeth tramps across the fields to join her and arrives in a bedraggled state.

❹ Elizabeth realises that the Bingley sisters have no real concern for Jane.

❺ Caroline Bingley tries to embarrass Elizabeth and run her down in Darcy's eyes.

❻ Mrs Bennet arrives with Lydia and embarrasses everyone by her rude and ignorant behaviour.

❼ Darcy refuses to join with the Bingley sisters in condemning Elizabeth and her family.

We learn more about Mr Bennet's circumstances and the fact that his estate and its income will pass to a distant relative. Mrs Bennet's inheritance is insufficient to support the daughters.

The two youngest daughters, Catherine (Kitty) and Lydia, on one of their regular visits to their aunt, Mrs Phillips, in nearby Meryton learn that an army regiment has set up camp nearby. They return home thrilled at the prospect of officers in their finest uniforms. Mr Bennet comments dryly on his daughters' silliness but Mrs Bennet, ever alert to the possibility of glamorous suitors, shares their enthusiasm.

CHECKPOINT 3
Make sure you understand what is meant by entailment and why it is important.

DID YOU KNOW?
Militias were garrisoned throughout England as a defence against invasion by Napoleon.

The excitement is interrupted by a message from Caroline Bingley inviting Jane to dine at Netherfield. Mrs Bennet is insistent that Jane should go on horseback, in the expectation that the onset of rain will enforce an overnight stay. News comes that, not only did the rain prevent Jane's immediate return, but that she has also fallen ill as a result of being soaked. Mrs Bennet is delighted at the prospect of an even longer stay at Netherfield. Concerned for her sister's health, Elizabeth makes her way to Netherfield across muddy fields, whilst Catherine and Lydia set off in search of officers. Bingley's sisters are contemptuous of Elizabeth's bedraggled state but Darcy quietly admires her fresh and healthy complexion. Jane's condition is felt to be sufficiently serious for Elizabeth to be invited to stay the night.

CHECK THE FILM

In the recent BBC adaptation (1996), Elizabeth is first seen out walking alone to emphasise her energetic, independent character.

Elizabeth senses that it is only Bingley who shows any true concern for Jane. His sisters, especially Caroline, are more concerned with impressing Mr Darcy. When she is upstairs tending Jane, they criticise her appearance, condemn her behaviour and are scornful of her family's low status and connections with trade. Darcy, however, confesses that he found Elizabeth's eyes even more attractive after her walk but concedes that the Bennet sisters' background is a significant handicap in marriage.

The evening is spent in a game of cards, which Elizabeth declines to join. Bingley goes out of his way to be kind to Elizabeth, while Miss Bingley continues to search for ways in which to embarrass or shame her. Elizabeth, however, is well able to hold her own and demonstrates her strength of mind and playful **wit** when she enters into a spirited conversation about what constitutes an 'accomplished' (Ch. 8, p. 35) woman. Miss Bingley suggests to Darcy that Elizabeth's modesty about her own skills is a cunning way of inviting praise. Darcy's reply, condemning deceit, seems directed more at Miss Bingley than Elizabeth. We learn that Jane is worse.

Mrs Bennet, accompanied by Catherine and Lydia, visits Jane, satisfies herself that the patient is not in danger, and then declares that she is far too ill to be moved. Mrs Bennet's rude and ignorant attempts at conversation are an embarrassment to everyone. She is uncivil to Darcy, and Elizabeth's attempts to change the subject lead only to Mrs Bennet's openly criticising Charlotte Lucas, whom she imagines to be a rival for Bingley's affections. Mrs Bennet's outburst is received in polite silence and Elizabeth is fearful that her mother might compromise herself further. However, she soon leaves, but not before Lydia brazenly reminds Bingley of his proposal to mount a ball, a promise he agrees to keep.

Left alone to talk of the morning's events, Mr Darcy refuses to agree with Miss Bingley's remarks about Elizabeth, despite her mother's appalling behaviour.

DID YOU KNOW?

In Jane Austen's day 'genteel' young women were expected to be 'accomplished', that is they should be able to draw, sing, play a musical instrumement and possibly speak a foreign language.

DID YOU KNOW?

When Lydia is described as 'stout' (Ch. 9, p. 40) it does not mean that she was fat but that she was in good health.

Challenging convention

By walking across the muddy fields, Elizabeth is prepared to be unconventional and unladylike for the sake of her sister. The Bingley sisters behave snobbishly towards Elizabeth but they conveniently forget that their wealth was made through trade and that they were not born into the gentry.

CHAPTER 10 – Rivalry

❶ Darcy tries to write a letter.

❷ Elizabeth engages in lively debate with Darcy.

❸ Elizabeth becomes aware of Darcy's gaze but rejects any thought that he may admire her.

❹ To Elizabeth's astonishment, Darcy offers to dance but she refuses because she imagines that he is being patronising.

❺ Darcy finds himself 'bewitched' (p. 46) by Elizabeth.

❻ Caroline shows her jealousy of Elizabeth by taunting Darcy with reminders of the Bennets' inferiority.

DID YOU KNOW?

Before the coming of the telegraph, letter writing was a particularly important activity. Jane Austen quotes twenty-one letters in *Pride and Prejudice*.

The evening proceeds quietly. Miss Bingley attaches herself to Darcy who is attempting to write a letter to his sister. To his irritation, she interrupts him with flattery at every turn. Eventually, the conversation opens up into a discussion of Bingley's impulsive and impressionable character. Elizabeth joins in and once again shows her spirit and quickness of thought. Unlike Darcy and Elizabeth, Bingley does not enjoy the cut and thrust of lively debate and brings the conversation to an end with a rough joke at Darcy's expense. Elizabeth realises that Darcy is 'rather offended' (p. 45) and tactfully smoothes over an awkward moment.

As Bingley's sisters play and sing at the piano, Elizabeth becomes aware of Darcy's gaze. The notion that she may be the object of his admiration crosses her mind, only to be dismissed immediately. She is taken back by his unexpected request for a dance. Believing him to be condescending and patronising, given his expressed distaste of dancing and of country living, she rejects his invitation with some force. She is surprised to note that Darcy displays no offence. In fact, he is so entranced by Elizabeth that he feels his only defence against her charms is the difference in their social rank.

Miss Bingley becomes increasingly jealous and tries to taunt Darcy with images of a demeaning future alliance with the Bennet family. Darcy refuses to rise to Caroline's bait but feels the Bingley sisters' rudeness when, during a walk in the grounds, they turn on to a path which is too narrow to allow Elizabeth to walk beside them.

CHAPTERS 11–12 – Darcy weakens

1 Jane, now recovered, joins the company and much to Elizabeth's pleasure is the constant object of Bingley's devoted attention.

2 Caroline once again tries to force her attentions on Darcy.

3 Elizabeth teases Darcy about his seriousness and goads him into admitting his pride and intolerance.

4 Darcy admires Elizabeth's readiness to argue with him and wonders whether he is becoming too attracted to her

Jane, restored to health, joins the ladies, who engage her in warm and agreeable conversation. However, as soon as the gentlemen enter, Caroline has eyes only for Darcy, while Bingley devotes all his attention to Jane, much to Elizabeth's approval. After tea, Miss Bingley, obviously bored, tries to distract Darcy from his reading but he makes no response until Elizabeth agrees to accompany Caroline on a walk about the room, at which point he looks up for the first time.

CHECKPOINT 4

Why do the Bingley sisters appear in good spirits at this time?

Darcy declines to join them and in the ensuing conversation Elizabeth teases him into admitting his dislike of being an object of fun. He claims it as a matter of pride that he has rid himself of any characteristic that may incur ridicule. Amused at his earnestness and self-regard, she further goads him into confessing that his character is too intolerant and unforgiving. He breaks off the conversation, smiling at Elizabeth's readiness to oppose him in argument. He is left wondering whether he is becoming too attracted to her and resolves 'that no sign of admiration should *now* escape him' (Ch. 12, p. 52).

The time has come for Jane and Elizabeth to leave, much to Darcy's relief, as he is becoming seriously concerned about the warmth of his feelings towards Elizabeth. During the remainder of the stay, they barely speak to one another. Jane's return is far too soon for her

CHECK THE BOOK

If you have the opportunity, try to compare Jane Austen's cool witty presentation of romantic relationships with the more passionate versions of some of her contemporaries such as the lovers Madeline and Porhyro in John Keats's poem, *The Eve of St Agnes* (1818), who are very different from Darcy and Elizabeth.

mother, but Mr Bennet is quietly glad to see his two elder daughters at home. Mary is deep in her musical studies and as for Catherine and Lydia, their heads are full of regimental nonsense.

The attraction begins

The episode at Netherfield is particularly important as it establishes the counteracting factors that draw Elizabeth and Darcy together and force them apart.

Elizabeth's three conversational encounters with Darcy, in which she is moved to provoke, tease and argue with him as an intellectual equal, suggest that her professed dislike is really unconscious fascination. Meanwhile, Darcy is becoming expressly attracted by Elizabeth's independent spirit and 'fine eyes' (Ch. 6, p. 25).

However, Miss Bingley's obvious jealousy of Elizabeth and Darcy's awareness of Elizabeth's social inferiority, accentuated by Mrs Bennet's vulgarity, are to prove major obstacles.

Now take a break!

ABOUT WHOM IS THIS SAID ...?

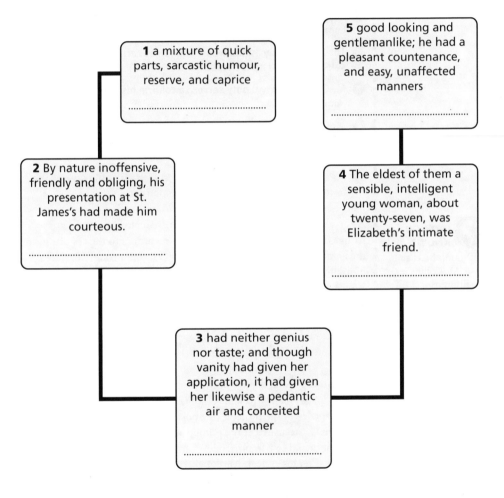

1 a mixture of quick parts, sarcastic humour, reserve, and caprice

....

5 good looking and gentlemanlike; he had a pleasant countenance, and easy, unaffected manners

....

2 By nature inoffensive, friendly and obliging, his presentation at St. James's had made him courteous.

....

4 The eldest of them a sensible, intelligent young woman, about twenty-seven, was Elizabeth's intimate friend.

....

3 had neither genius nor taste; and though vanity had given her application, it had given her likewise a pedantic air and conceited manner

....

Check your answers on p. 113.

CHAPTERS 13–14 – Mr Collins presents himself

1 Mr Bennet receives a letter from Mr Collins to whom the Longbourn estate is entailed.

2 The letter boldly announces his imminent arrival and is totally self-regarding and tactless.

3 Mr Collins's arrival only serves to confirm his vulgarity and pomposity.

4 Mr Collins bathes in the reflected glory of his patron, Lady Catherine de Bourgh and reveals that her daughter is intended to marry Mr Darcy.

5 Mr Bennet takes every opportunity to feed Mr Collins the chance to reveal his absurd sense of self-importance.

DID YOU KNOW?

Although he is a fool, Mr Collins qualifies as a member of the gentry because he is a clergyman.

At breakfast the following morning, Mr Bennet produces a letter from a distant cousin, Mr Collins, who according to the conditions of the entail, will inherit Longbourn estate. Having proudly declared himself a clergyman enjoying the patronage of Lady Catherine de Bourgh he announces his arrival at Longbourn that very day, Monday 18 November, and his intention to stay until the following Saturday. He claims his purpose is to make peace with the Bennet family and there is a hint that he might 'make every possible amends' (Ch. 13, p. 55) for any injustice by marrying one of the daughters.

Mrs Bennet's initial dismay at the prospect of meeting the 'odious' (Ch. 13, p. 54) man who will rob the children of their inheritance is soon dispelled at the thought of a possible marriage. Elizabeth, however, is astonished at the pomposity of the letter and its mixture of 'servility and self-importance' (Ch. 13, p. 56), a view that is confirmed on his arrival. At dinner that evening, he vulgarly talks of how Mrs Bennet's daughters should be 'well disposed of in marriage' (Ch. 13, p. 57) and apologises at excessive length for suggesting that one of them might have performed the role of cook.

CHECKPOINT 5

Why should Mr Collins's suggestion that one of the sisters might have cooked the meal cause offence?

As the evening progresses Mr Collins proves to be an entirely ridiculous figure. His gratitude to Lady Catherine is unrestrained and he even reveals that it was she who suggested that he should marry.

He is also wholly complimentary about Lady Cath rine's daughter, Miss de Bourgh, who we learn later in the novel, is intended to marry Mr Darcy. However, although he describes her as 'charming … born to be a duchess' (Ch. 14, p. 59), Mr Collins cannot disguise the fact that she is an unattractive, sickly girl of little accomplishment.

Mr Bennet is highly amused at Mr Collins's pomposity and 'feeds' his visitor the chance to display his self-importance. His solemn sense of superiority is further emphasised when he proclaims surprise that young ladies such as Lydia should prefer works of fiction to morally improving sermons. He spends the remainder of the evening playing backgammon.

CHECKPOINT 6

What does his words to Lydia and his pleasure at backgammon reveal of Mr Collins's true character?

Mr Collins

Once encountered, it is impossible to forget Mr Collins. Jane Austen's skill in presenting this absurd character has much to do with her ability to make him consistent. He is entirely predictable; everything he says or does, down to the last detail, reinforces the picture of smug pomposity combined with sickening servility. The way he speaks is indistinguishable from the way he writes in its cumbersome expression and its utter insensitivity.

GLOSSARY
odious hateful, repulsive

CHAPTERS 15–17 – A glamorous stranger

❶ Mr Collins is in search of a wife; his first choice is Jane but on learning of her likely engagement, he immediately switches his attention to Elizabeth.

❷ The Bennet sisters go to Meryton where they are introduced to a charming stranger, Mr Wickham.

❸ When Bingley and Darcy arrive on horseback, Elizabeth notices that Darcy and Wickham are clearly surprised and embarrassed to encounter one another.

❹ Elizabeth is charmed by Wickham and is shocked when he reveals that Darcy denied him his rightful entitlement to a living.

❺ Elizabeth tells her elder sister what she has learned but Jane refuses to blame anyone.

❻ The invitation to the ball at Netherfield arrives; Elizabeth 'thought with pleasure of dancing a good deal with Mr. Wickham' (Ch. 17, p. 74).

We are told of Mr Collins's background. We learn that for all his self-proclaimed pride in his own virtues and his readiness to be associated with aristocracy, he came from a narrow background, was lazy at university and extremely lucky to gain the prosperous living at Hunsford. As an eligible bachelor and convinced of his generosity towards the Bennet family, he has come to Longbourn to marry one of the daughters. His first choice is the most obviously beautiful daughter, Jane, but on learning from Mrs Bennet of her likely engagement, he immediately switches his attention to Elizabeth. Mrs Bennet is predictably delighted at the thought of shortly having two married daughters.

DID YOU KNOW?

A gentleman's library was often regarded as a personal and private place that one did not enter uninvited.

Mr Bennet, irritated that the privacy of his library should be invaded by Mr Collins, who is not the least interested in reading, recommends that he should accompany the sisters on a walk to Meryton.

When they arrive, the sisters are introduced by an officer acquaintance of Kitty and Lydia to a handsome and charming stranger, Mr Wickham. At that moment, Bingley and Darcy arrive on horseback and, seeing the sisters, promptly make towards the company assembled in the street. Elizabeth is startled and overcome with curiosity when she notices that Darcy and Wickham are clearly surprised and deeply embarrassed to encounter each other.

The sisters and Mr Collins progress to their aunt's. Mrs Philips and Mr Collins indulge in exchanging exaggerated civilities. An invitation is extended to dine at the Philips' that evening with the possibility of Mr Wickham being in attendance.

When they return in the evening, accompanied by Mr Collins, the girls are delighted to hear that Mr Wickham has accepted Mr Philips's invitation to dinner. Settled in his place, Mr Collins continues to flatter Mrs Philips by comparing her drawing room favourably with Lady Catherine's 'small summer' (Ch. 16, p. 65) breakfast parlour. The girls' boredom at hearing Mr Collins's catalogue the wonders of Lady Catherine's mansion is relieved with the appearance of Wickham and the other gentlemen.

The normally level-headed Elizabeth is immediately won over by Wickham's easy, outgoing manner and his charming conversation. Elizabeth's curiosity about the relationship between Wickham and Darcy is soon answered. Unprompted, Wickham enquires after Darcy's whereabouts, plans and Elizabeth's acquaintance with him.

? DID YOU KNOW?
In Jane Austen's day, as now, people often tried to impress others by their wealth. To spend £800 on a fireplace was a sign of conspicuous extravagance.

<table>
<tr><td>

CHECKPOINT 7

Why is Elizabeth
so ready to believe
Wickham's story?

</td><td>

Elizabeth readily expresses her dislike of Darcy, and Wickham appears
to take her into his confidence by giving an account of his past history.
Wickham's father had been a loyal employee of Darcy's father who in
turn had taken the young Wickham under his wing. He had promised

</td></tr>
</table>

Wickham a career in the church with the certainty of the appointment
to a desirable living. Mr Darcy, however, had gone back on his father's
promise and given the living to another. Elizabeth is shocked at such
an injustice but impressed when Wickham declares that he can never
expose Darcy out of respect for his father. Even so, she cannot
understand how Darcy could have acted so heartlessly. Wickham's
explanation is that Darcy is jealous of his late father's affection for
Wickham and has come to thoroughly dislike him as a result.
Wickham agrees with Elizabeth that Darcy is motivated by pride and
goes on to suggest that his generosity and good deeds stem from
excessive pride in his reputation rather than from sincere concern for
others. His treatment of Wickham, however, is a result of even
'stronger impulses' (Ch. 16, p. 70).

When Elizabeth wonders how such an amiable person as Bingley
could enjoy the company of such a disagreeable man as Darcy,
Wickham replies that Darcy can be pleasant when it suits him.
Overhearing mention of Lady Catherine de Bourgh, Wickham
explains to Elizabeth that she is Mr Darcy's aunt and that Miss de
Bourgh and Darcy are believed to be due to marry. Elizabeth is
amused at the thought of Miss Bingley's designs on Darcy being
thwarted and she is pleased that Wickham is able to confirm her view
that Lady Catherine must be an arrogant woman.

As Elizabeth returns home her head is full of thoughts of Wickham
and his revelations.

<table>
<tr><td>

CHECKPOINT 8

Why is Jane's
refusal to blame
both her strength
and her weakness?

</td><td>

The next day Elizabeth tells Jane about what she has learned.
Characteristically, Jane refuses to attribute blame to either Darcy or
Wickham, although privately she is concerned whether Bingley really
has been used by Darcy. Elizabeth is convinced that Wickham was
telling the truth.

</td></tr>
</table>

An invitation to the planned ball at Netherfield arrives which moves
Elizabeth to dream of dancing with Wickham. Unfortunately, out of

politeness, she is obliged to agree to Mr Collins's offer to share the first two dances. In fact, she comes to realise that Mr Collins has chosen her to be his wife but she ignores her mother's support for the idea. The week drags. The rain prevents any excursions to Meryton. Only the prospect of the ball offers the girls any relief.

CHECK THE BOOK

Wuthering Heights (1847) is another novel by a clergyman's daughter (Emily Brontë) but it is much more passionate and brooding.

Mr Wickham

Wickham is to all appearances everything that Mr Collins is not: handsome, charming, well spoken and approachable. The **irony** is that they are both equally lacking in moral scruples, both wholly mercenary and both prepared to exploit women. Wickham, however, has more in common with the totally immoral, sweet-talking villains of **romantic fiction**

Elizabeth's curiosity and eagerness to soak up any scandal concerning the 'hate figure' Darcy, causes her to overlook Wickham's overfamiliarity and lack of propriety. She is also prepared to excuse Wickham's absence (see Chapter 18) from the one ball she had been looking forward to as evidence of his tact, rather than as deliberate avoidance of Darcy. She later appreciates Darcy's sense of honour and discretion in not talking freely about Wickham.

CHAPTER 18 – Elizabeth's hopes are dashed

1 Elizabeth is deeply disappointed when Wickham is nowhere to be seen at the ball.

2 Elizabeth agrees to dance with Darcy and when he becomes distant on the mention of Wickham, she is convinced that Wickham was telling the truth.

3 Darcy privately forgives Elizabeth but can feel nothing but anger towards Wickham.

4 Elizabeth is once again embarrassed by her family's vulgar behaviour.

At the Netherfield ball Elizabeth is disappointed from the outset; she searches in vain for Wickham, only to be told that he is absent. She suspects Darcy to be responsible. She is surprised and irritated when she finds herself accepting Darcy's offer of a dance. Charlotte Lucas warns her not to allow her liking for Wickham to offend a man of such importance as Mr Darcy. As they dance, Elizabeth tries unsuccessfully to probe Darcy concerning Wickham. Darcy becomes distant when she raises the matter and although he is impeccably polite, it is clear that he wishes to change the subject. Elizabeth can only believe that Wickham was telling the truth but not before she and Darcy have had a lively conversation which touches on the mysteries of Darcy's character. Furthermore, she considers Miss Bingley's warning not to believe Wickham as 'insolent' (p. 81) and she even discounts Jane's assurances of Bingley's trust in Darcy's integrity. For his part, Darcy privately forgives Elizabeth but feels nothing but anger towards Wickham.

DID YOU KNOW?

It was considered a breach of etiquette in polite society to enter into a conversation, especially with a person of superior rank, without a formal introduction.

Letting the side down

The behaviour of members of Elizabeth's family at the Netherfield ball displays a crassness and lack of refinement that only serves to feed Darcy's sense of their inferiority. Elizabeth is embarrassed because her own sense of decency and decorum is offended, but the scene also foreshadows her later shame at her family's even more serious deficiencies and her despair at what she thinks must be Darcy's justifiable reactions.

The remainder of the evening proves a protracted source of shame for Elizabeth as she is forced to witness the embarrassing behaviour of members of her family. First, Mr Collins, ignoring Elizabeth's protestations and oblivious of etiquette, forces his fawning attentions on Mr Darcy who receives him with polite astonishment. Secondly, her mother talks brazenly to Lady Lucas about her confidence in the impending marriage of Jane to Mr Bingley and loudly disparages Mr Darcy, all within his earshot. Elizabeth is convinced that he has been listening. Thirdly, Mary's attempts at entertaining the company in song are so feeble as to find Elizabeth 'in agonies' (p. 85). Then, to the amazement of half the room, Mr Collins loudly delivers a speech on his duties as a clergyman, the first of which he declares, is to secure his personal income. Finally, Mrs Bennet contrives to be the last to leave and Elizabeth has to endure the embarrassed silence in which her mother's chatter and Mr Collins's speeches were received.

CHAPTERS 19–21 – Mr Collins proposes

1 Mr Collins proposes to Elizabeth; he refuses to believe that Elizabeth means what she says when she turns him down.

2 Elizabeth is well able to resist her mother's attempts to talk her around.

3 Mr Bennet refuses to intervene and eventually Mr Collins withdraws his offer.

4 When Charlotte Lucas enters Mr Collins pays her a great deal of close attention.

5 News arrives of the departure of the entire Netherfield party for London.

As time is short before his return to Hunsford Parsonage, Mr Collins decides to propose. Mrs Bennet readily agrees to his request for an audience with her daughter and excitedly scurries upstairs leaving Elizabeth to face Mr Collins.

Even by the conventions of the day, his proposal is excessively formal and consists entirely of reasons why *he* should marry. He makes clear that he is bestowing an honour on the Bennet household. When Elizabeth refuses him with all the civility she can summon, Mr Collins flatters himself that she is merely being coy. Her continued resistance fails to shake his conviction that she will eventually accept, although he does warn her that she may not receive another such an offer of marriage. Eventually, Elizabeth leaves it to her father to convince Mr Collins that she really does not want to marry him.

Mrs Bennet is distressed on hearing of Elizabeth's refusal but reassures Mr Collins that Mr Bennet will talk her round.

Mr Bennet, however, derives wry amusement from the situation and

EXAMINER'S SECRET
It is always a good idea to collect a range of words to describe a character. Mr Collins is 'pompous' but he is lots of other things beside; you'll find other adjectives in these Notes.

CHECK THE BOOK

Barbara Pym's *Some Tame Gazelle* which was published in 1950 contains a proposal of marriage from a pompous and ridiculous clergyman!

refuses to intervene. After much distracted pleading and cajoling on Mrs Bennet's part, which Elizabeth rather enjoys rebutting, Mr Collins withdraws his offer as ponderously and wordily as he had made it. Significantly, Charlotte Lucas has entered and is the subject of Mr Collins's close attention.

In the aftermath of Elizabeth's refusal, Mrs Bennet's continues to be bad-tempered while Mr Collins maintains a 'resentful silence' (Ch. 21, p. 97) towards Elizabeth. He shows no lack of lengthy civility to Charlotte, however.

Elizabeth meets Wickham once more in Meryton and admires his tact when he explains that he chose to stay away from the ball in order to avoid Darcy. She is flattered when Wickham and an officer friend accompany the sisters home.

When they arrive home, Jane receives a letter from Miss Bingley announcing their sudden return to London. Jane is naturally distressed and is particularly hurt by Miss Bingley's suggestion that Darcy's sister, Georgiana, is a fine prospect for the hand of Bingley. Elizabeth, however, is confident of Bingley's attachment to Jane and attributes his sister's suggestions to malice and wishful thinking. Jane cannot accept that Caroline could be so devious and, despite Elizabeth's reassurances concerning his independent spirit, despairs of Bingley's early return.

CHAPTERS 22–3 – Mr Collins succeeds at the second attempt

❶ Charlotte accepts Mr Collins's proposal of marriage.

❷ Elizabeth is shocked and feels that her friend has disgraced herself.

❸ Lady Lucas is triumphant and Mrs Bennet totally put out. Elizabeth feels that a barrier has come between her and Charlotte.

❹ Jane is quietly distressed because there seems little prospect of Bingley's return.

Elizabeth is grateful that Charlotte has taken on the burden of entertaining Mr Collins but cannot suspect that her friend is hopeful that he will propose to her. Before long he does just that and she readily accepts. She is under no illusions concerning Mr Collins's character but the prospect of financial security outweighs any thoughts of romance or affection: 'I am not romantic you know. I never was. I ask only a comfortable home' (Ch. 22, p. 105). Elizabeth is shocked and disappointed when Charlotte breaks the news to her in private, feeling that her friend has disgraced herself.

When Sir William tells the rest of the Bennet family of the engagement, they react in predictable ways. When the truth has sunk in, Mrs Bennet becomes entirely unnerved and blames Elizabeth for ruining her chances of marrying off one of her daughters. Mr Bennet derives perverse satisfaction from the thought he is not uniquely blessed with the company of foolish women. Jane is surprised but wishes the couple happiness. Elizabeth feels that a barrier has come between herself and her friend and is drawn closer to her elder sister. For Kitty and Lydia the news is merely a subject for gossip as Mr Collins is 'only a clergyman' (Ch. 23, p. 107).

> ### CHECKPOINT 9
> How is Mrs Bennet's reaction to the news of Charlotte's engagement typical of her character?

Meanwhile, Jane has been awaiting news of the Bingleys but as the days pass the two sisters become more anxious, especially as there is a rumour that Bingley will not return that winter. Even Elizabeth's trust in Bingley's determination begins to weaken and she wonders whether he has been influenced by his sisters and Darcy.

Mrs Bennet's misery is compounded by the thought that Charlotte will one day supplant her as mistress of Longbourn.

 DID YOU KNOW?
Mr Collins was, in fact, a rector which meant he was in a senior position among parish clergy and guaranteed a significant income, besides inheriting Longbourn.

> ### One view of marriage
> Charlotte's engagement sets the seal on one important view of marriage. Elizabeth is shocked and disappointed for reasons of integrity. Mrs Bennet is shocked, disappointed and full of recrimination because a golden opportunity has slipped through their fingers. The Lucases see the engagement as a triumph. For the moment, the sentiment of the novel's opening sentence seems amply justified.

Who says ...?

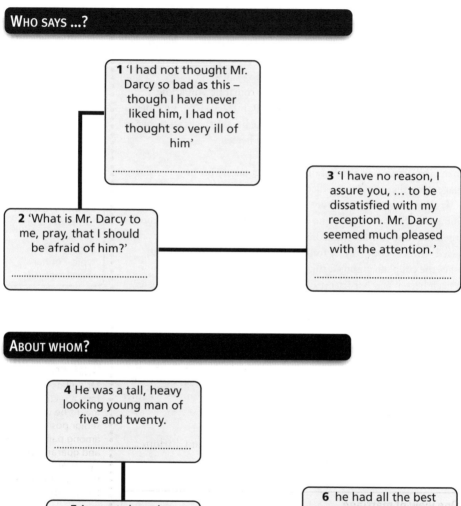

1 'I had not thought Mr. Darcy so bad as this – though I have never liked him, I had not thought so very ill of him'

....

3 'I have no reason, I assure you, ... to be dissatisfied with my reception. Mr. Darcy seemed much pleased with the attention.'

....

2 'What is Mr. Darcy to me, pray, that I should be afraid of him?'

....

About whom?

4 He was a tall, heavy looking young man of five and twenty.

....

5 'a most charming young lady indeed ... [but] ... unfortunately of a sickly constitution'

....

6 he had all the best part of beauty, a fine countenance, a good figure, and very pleasing address

....

Check your answers on p. 113.

CHAPTERS 24–6 – Disappointment for Jane

❶ Jane despairs when she receives confirmation that the Bingleys intend to remain in London.

❷ Elizabeth suspects the interference of the Bingley sisters and Darcy.

❸ The Gardiners come to stay and invite Jane to their home in London.

❹ Mrs Gardiner becomes uneasy at Wickham's warm relationship with Elizabeth.

❺ Elizabeth assures her aunt that she is not in love with Wickham.

❻ Jane goes to London and sees Miss Bingley only briefly. Jane admits that Elizabeth was right about Caroline's deceitful character.

❼ Wickham turns his attention towards Miss King. Elizabeth convinces herself that she feels no resentment.

Now he has departed, Jane cannot but feel that her relationship with Bingley is at an end, especially as Caroline stresses his affection for Miss Darcy, but she resigns herself to the situation with her usual serenity. Elizabeth is more critical, suspecting that her sister's happiness has been ruined by the influences of the Bingley sisters and Darcy. Jane is ready to see the best in everyone, even those who have been the cause of hurt, but Elizabeth has come to take a more negative view of human character as she continues to be astonished at Charlotte's engagement to 'a conceited, pompous, narrow-minded, silly man' (Ch. 24, p. 115). Elizabeth shows a keener awareness of people's motives than Jane but accepts Wickham at face value.

With his usual tongue-in-cheek cynicism, Mr Bennet sees that at least Jane has achieved an enviable status for having been crossed in love. Furthermore, he suggests that Elizabeth should emulate her sister by encouraging Wickham, who would jilt her 'creditably' (Ch. 24, p. 116). The less sympathetic side to Mr Bennet begins to emerge. His treatment of Jane's disappointment as a fortunate circumstance shows his readiness to reduce everything to a joke. By this time Wickham has become generally accepted as one who has suffered at Mr Darcy's hands. **Ironically**, only Jane considers that there may be another side to the story.

CHECKPOINT 10

Why is Mr Bennet's joke about Wickham jilting Elizabeth ironic?

Mrs Bennet's brother and sister-in-law, the Gardiners, come to stay. They are a pleasant and sensible couple and Mrs Gardiner is a particular favourite of Jane and Elizabeth. On the subject of Jane's disappointment, she is somewhat dubious of the true sincerity of Bingley's passions but sympathises with the hurt that Jane must feel. Elizabeth is delighted when Jane is invited to stay with the Gardiners in London and secretly harbours the slim hope Bingley might yet find Jane's nearness impossible to resist.

CHECKPOINT 11

Why is Mrs Gardiner's remembrance of Mr Darcy misleading?

When Mrs Gardiner meets Wickham she feels some disquiet at his intimacy with Elizabeth but enjoys talking to him about Pemberley and Mr Darcy's father. By way of confirming the general opinion of Mr Darcy, she dimly remembers him being reported as 'a very proud, ill-natured boy' (Ch. 25, p. 121).

Mrs Gardiner warns Elizabeth about becoming too attracted to Wickham. He is good company but has no fortune. Elizabeth reassures her aunt that although she is much taken by him – she declares him to be 'the most agreeable man' she ever saw, in contrast to '*that* abominable Mr Darcy!' (Ch. 26, p. 122) – she is not in love but cannot be entirely responsible for how her feelings may develop.

Mr Collins and Charlotte are married. Elizabeth promises to visit Charlotte in Kent but feels that their friendship will never be quite the same again.

 DID YOU KNOW?

Charlotte settles about 50 miles away which for an experienced traveller like Darcy is '*a very* easy distance' (Ch. 32, p. 148). But for Elizabeth who has never left the area it is not at all near.

Jane writes that she has paid an all too brief visit to Caroline Bingley but that she expects an early return visit. A month passes before Caroline comes to see Jane. Caroline's offhand behaviour finally leads Jane reluctantly to acknowledge that Elizabeth was right about Caroline's deceitful character.

Meanwhile, Wickham has turned his attentions on a certain Miss King, a wealthy young heiress. Elizabeth convinces herself that she feels no disappointment and accepts Wickham's desire for financial security.

The Gardiners

The Gardiners represent honesty, good sense and true gentility. It is interesting that they enter the story just at the point that Caroline Bingley's lack of these qualities are clearly demonstrated in her treatment of Jane.

CHAPTERS 27–8 – A change of scene

① It is March. Accompanied by Sir William Lucas Elizabeth sets out to visit Charlotte in Kent, breaking her journey at the Gardiners' in London.

② Elizabeth defends Wickham against the charge of being money-grabbing.

③ Mrs Gardiner proposes a summer tour of England.

 DID YOU KNOW?

It was not considered proper for a woman to travel unaccompanied.

4 In Hunsford Mr Collins delights in showing off all the comforts and delights of the parsonage, pointedly trying to make her regret refusing his proposal.

5 Next morning Elizabeth catches sight of Miss de Bourgh.

6 The whole party is asked to dine at Rosings.

When Elizabeth is in London, Mrs Gardiner questions Wickham's motives for his sudden interest in Miss King. Elizabeth defends him against the charge of being mercenary but cannot avoid sounding generally depressed and disillusioned. In order to raise her niece's spirits, the Gardiners propose she join them on an extensive tour of England that summer.

Much cheered by seeing her sister and the Gardiners' invitation, Elizabeth continues her journey to Hunsford. Mr Collins is as appalling as ever but Charlotte appears entirely contented with her new home. The next morning Elizabeth is called to the window to witness Miss de Bourgh sitting in her carriage talking to Charlotte. She deplores her rudeness in keeping Charlotte standing outside in the cold March winds but takes a mischievous delight in the thought that Darcy is destined to marry such an ill-tempered, sickly creature: 'I like her appearance …. She looks sickly and cross …. She will make him a proper wife.' (Ch. 28, p. 132–3).

CHECKPOINT 12

What does Elizabeth's reaction to the sight of Miss de Bourgh, tell us of her feelings towards Darcy?

CHAPTERS 29–30 – Awful Lady Catherine

1 Mr Collins is extravagant in his praise of Rosings; Sir William and his daughter are awe-struck, but Elizabeth is entirely at ease.

2 Lady Catherine is as arrogant as Elizabeth expects.

3 Elizabeth stands up to Lady Catherine.

4 Elizabeth appreciates how Charlotte has organised her living arrangements.

5 Mr Darcy and his cousin, Colonel Fitzwilliam, visit their aunt at Rosings.

The next day the whole party dines at Lady Catherine's mansion, Rosings. Elizabeth is soon able to observe Lady Catherine soaking up endless compliments from Mr Collins and Sir William and behaving in as arrogant, patronising and dictatorial manner as she had imagined. Elizabeth feels particularly insulted by Lady Catherine's impertinent questions about her family but she manages to remain polite. At one point, however, Elizabeth bridles at being rudely asked her age. Lady Catherine's evident surprise at her refusal to give a direct reply, prompts Elizabeth to speculate that she may be the first person to stand up to her Ladyship.

The days pass routinely. Elizabeth appreciates how Charlotte has organised her living arrangements to avoid continuous contact with her husband and she sees that Lady Catherine's officiousness extends to interfering in the lives of the local villagers and tenants.

News comes that Mr Darcy and his cousin, Colonel Fitzwilliam, are to visit their aunt at Rosings. Despite her feelings towards Darcy, Elizabeth welcomes the prospect of new company. The gentlemen pay a surprisingly early courtesy call on the Collins which Charlotte believes is entirely due to Elizabeth's presence. Darcy says little but appears confused when Elizabeth mentions that Jane 'has been in town these three months' (Ch. 30, p. 142). Darcy's immediate visit indicates his continuing interest in Elizabeth.

EXAMINER'S SECRET

You will gain marks if you can make comparisons, such as the differences between Darcy's and Lady Catherine's 'pride'.

CHECKPOINT 13

What is suggested by the fact that Darcy and his cousin visit Hunsford so soon after their arrival?

Ladylike Lady Catherine?

Elizabeth's readiness to resist Lady Catherine's overbearing manner anticipates later developments.

Lady Catherine's close questioning of Elizabeth about her family shows her impertinence and readiness to interfere in others' affairs, in her own way she is as vulgar and tactless as Mrs Bennet. Her treatment of the local community contrasts sharply with Darcy's (see Chapter 43).

Lady Catherine represents the old aristocracy at its worst: rich but devoid of taste; privileged but insolent; powerful but irresponsible. Lady Catherine has the social status but lacks the attendant values; Elizabeth lacks the status but displays a superior sense of values.

CHAPTERS 31–2 – Darcy shows his interest

❶ Elizabeth is invited to Rosings and is admired by Darcy.

❷ Lady Catherine criticises Elizabeth's piano playing.

❸ Next morning, Elizabeth is surprised by the sudden appearance of Mr Darcy, alone.

❹ Charlotte is convinced that Darcy is in love with Elizabeth.

On a visit to Rosings, Elizabeth is charmed by Colonel Fitzwilliam and Darcy is quick to observe their warm conversation. Lady Catherine dominates proceedings as usual and her patronising attitude towards Elizabeth embarrasses Darcy. She criticises her playing, comparing it with the high standard her daughter *might* have achieved had she been in good health. Elizabeth watches Darcy's reaction but is unable to discern any signs of love towards Miss de Bourgh. When Elizabeth begins to sing, Darcy moves over to the piano so that he can observe her more closely. A lively conversation ensues in which Elizabeth provocatively charges Darcy with being an unsociable person, to which he replies that he is always shy in strange company.

The next morning, Darcy appears unexpectedly while Elizabeth is sitting alone in the parsonage. They engage in a strained conversation and Darcy will not be drawn on the subject of Bingley's rapid departure from Netherfield. At one point, however, he appears to suggest surprise that Elizabeth could possibly be satisfied with such a narrow society as offered by Longbourn.

When Charlotte returns she is tempted to believe that Darcy is falling in love with Elizabeth. Elizabeth dismisses the idea but Charlotte continues to wonder at the frequency of the two gentlemen's visits, for she has also noticed how Colonel Fitzwilliam and Elizabeth enjoy each other's company. She has observed Darcy's admiring glances at Elizabeth and in her own mind, she decides that he would make the more desirable husband of the two. She feels certain that 'her friend's dislike would vanish, if she could suppose him in her power' (Ch. 32, p. 150).

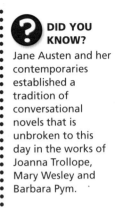

DID YOU KNOW?

Jane Austen and her contemporaries established a tradition of conversational novels that is unbroken to this day in the works of Joanna Trollope, Mary Wesley and Barbara Pym.

CHAPTER 33 – Elizabeth learns some shocking news

1 Elizabeth is surprised at how frequently she and Darcy meet when she wanders along the estate's paths.

2 She meets Colonel Fitzwilliam and is shocked when she learns that Darcy has intervened to save Bingley from a 'most imprudent marriage' (p. 153).

Elizabeth chooses to walk on the estate's least frequented paths, and she is surprised at how often she meets Darcy. During her walk with Colonel Fitzwilliam she suspects he is referring to the relationship between Mr Bingley and Jane. Elizabeth feels angry and indignant that Darcy's arrogance and pride have destroyed her sister's happiness. She also takes Darcy's actions as a personal slight because she suspects that he was influenced less by her mother's lack of social graces than by the Bennet family's lack of connections. She feels unwell and is unable to attend Rosings that evening.

GLOSSARY
imprudent inappropriate; unwise

Changing feelings

Chapters 31–3 are relatively quiet and free of incident but they reveal conflicting aspects of Elizabeth's feelings. Away from the distractions of her family and the interfering Miss Bingley, she clearly relishes the cut and thrust of conversation with Darcy whose repeated visits moves Charlotte to declare, 'My dear Eliza he must be in love with you, or he would never have called on us in this familiar way' (Ch. 32, p. 149). Within the conventions of the time her almost playful teasing and Darcy's admission of discomfort among strangers reach beyond the limits of formal politeness. In addition, Darcy and Elizabeth feel a like-minded embarrassment at Lady Catherine's overbearing vulgarity.

Against this *unconscious* sympathy, one must set Elizabeth's *conscious* antagonism towards Darcy because she believes that, as a result of his pride, he has ruined her sister's life.

CHAPTER 34 – Bombshell

CHECKPOINT 14

How does the scene at Rosings lay the ground for the effects of Lady Catherine's attempts to prevent the marriage of Darcy and Elizabeth?

❶ Elizabeth rereads Jane's letters and concludes that her sister is truly depressed at which point Darcy himself appears at the door.

❷ Darcy confesses his admiration for her and proposes marriage.

❸ Elizabeth's response is heated; she accuses Darcy of ruining her sister's life.

❹ Darcy admits intervening in Bingley's affairs but claims it would be dishonest not to have done so.

❺ When Elizabeth accuses Darcy of not acting like a gentleman he is taken aback and soon after leaves.

❻ Elizabeth is confused.

Rereading Jane's letters, Elizabeth concludes that her sister is truly depressed. Darcy enters and, after a few polite enquires after her health, suddenly declares his love and proposes marriage, making clear that his passion has fought with his awareness of her social inferiority.

Elizabeth's reply is candid. She regards his account of how he had overcome his natural prejudice towards her social position as 'uncivil' (p. 158). She also accuses him of ruining her sister's life and being the source of Wickham's misfortunes. Darcy protests that he was merely being frank and it would have been dishonest of him not to admit his concerns about their respective social standing.

CHECKPOINT 15

Which of Elizabeth's accusations do you think prompts Darcy to leave?

Elizabeth fiercely retorts that the manner of his proposal was ungentlemanly and she proceeds to accuse him of being arrogant, self-centred and uncaring of the feelings of others. Darcy is hurt, politely wishes her well and leaves. Elizabeth is left in a state of total bewilderment. She is full of indignation at the man's 'abominable pride' (p. 160) but in a strange way she also feels flattered that a man of Darcy's distinction should have proposed to her.

CHAPTERS 35–6 – Elizabeth begins to think again

① Out for her walk the following day, Elizabeth cannot avoid Darcy who hands her a letter and promptly withdraws.

② The letter is long and explains his actions concerning Bingley and Wickham.

DID YOU KNOW?

It was not considered proper for unmarried men and women to correspond with each other. That is why Darcy hands Elizabeth the letter and she does not reply.

In his letter to Elizabeth, Darcy makes no apology for detaching Bingley from Jane. He explains that the difference in social station might have been bridged but her family's 'want of propriety' (Ch. 35, p. 163) could not be excused. Jane and Elizabeth, however, were excused this charge. Darcy also remarks that Jane's lack of any obvious outward response to Bingley's attentions influenced his assessment of the affair. Darcy, however, does admit to a perhaps unworthy deception in concealing Jane's presence in London.

On the subject of Wickham, he accepts that Elizabeth could not possibly have guessed the truth. Wickham is a wastrel, who had given up any claim on the church living he had been promised, preferring to accept from Darcy three thousand pounds, on the pretext of studying for the law. When the money ran out, he returned to demand that Darcy present him with the living. When Darcy refused, Wickham showed nothing but resentment. Worst of all, Wickham tried to seduce and elope with Darcy's sister; she was just fifteen. His motive could only have been revenge and the attractions of Miss Darcy's thirty thousand pounds. Darcy ends by recommending Elizabeth to Colonel Fitzwilliam if confirmation of these details were needed.

DID YOU KNOW?

In Jane Austen's day a secure position in the church was much sought after – perhaps the equivalent of a senior managerial post today. Is Wickham unsuited to such employment?

Elizabeth's first reaction is to reject Darcy's account out of hand. His attitude toward Jane is insulting and confirms his arrogance, whilst the account of Wickham's character produces nothing but feelings of horror. On reflection, however, she begins to realise how prejudiced and self-deluding she has been. She wonders how she could possibly have overlooked Wickham's indiscretion in talking as he did at their first meeting. Casting her mind back, she realises that nothing was known about Wickham and there is no evidence to support the high opinion in which he is held. She now appreciates his cowardice in avoiding Darcy by not attending the Netherfield ball and in criticising him publicly when he had left the district.

CHECKPOINT 16

What remarks of Charlotte does Elizabeth remember?

She cannot blame Darcy for his impressions of her sister, which only confirm Charlotte's concern about Jane's failure to show her true feelings. Furthermore, she is painfully aware of her family's lack of breeding and can take little comfort from Darcy's compliments concerning Jane and herself.

A turning point

Darcy's proposal and letter of explanation come at a central point in the novel and signal a turning point.

Darcy's proposal could not be more unfortunately timed, so incensed is Elizabeth at what she believes is the ruin of Jane's chances of happiness. However, the **irony** is that her intense anger prompts her to step beyond the bounds of etiquette (she is far more polite to the foolish Mr Collins) and accuse Darcy of ungentlemanly behaviour. We learn later that it was this charge that made Darcy re-examine his motives. Even so, in the midst of her indignation is the faintest hint of romantic stirring, when she briefly allows herself to feel flattered that one such as Darcy should have proposed to her.

Darcy's letter sets Elizabeth thinking. Her clear-sighted analysis of the letter confirms her intelligence and her willingness to see another's **point of view**. It also rather sets her somewhat apart from her family whom she loves but whose actions she cannot always justify.

EXAMINER'S SECRET

A sign of a good candidate is the ability to cross-reference, e.g. to provide evidence of Elizabeth's misjudgement of Darcy from different parts of the novel.

CHAPTERS 37–8 – Departure

❶ Darcy and Colonel Fitzwilliam leave and Elizabeth prepares to return home.

❷ As she thinks about what he has revealed, her opinion of Darcy changes almost completely.

❸ She takes leave of her hosts leaving Charlotte to 'her home and her housekeeping, her parish and her poultry' (Ch. 8, p. 178).

The gentlemen have departed and despite Lady Catherine's protestations Elizabeth is planning to return home. In the remaining days, she gives much thought to Darcy's letter and her anger towards him begins to turn to respect. She cannot defend her family from his criticisms; 'they were hopeless of remedy' (Ch. 37, p. 175). Even her

GLOSSARY

propriety 'correct' behaviour

Chapters 37–8 continued

**CHECK
THE FILM**

In the recent BBC
adaptation (1996)
the content of
Darcy's letter is
conveyed partly
through dramatic
illustration, partly
through voice-over.
Notice what can be
dramatised and
what cannot.

father cannot escape rebuke. He has failed to control the moody
Catherine and the flirtatious Lydia, whose excesses have been
encouraged by an irresponsible mother. Elizabeth cannot escape the
truth that her family are responsible for Jane's misfortunes.

Elizabeth takes her leave of Charlotte and Mr Collins and travels the
short distance to London. Jane is to return with her to Longbourn.

Now take a break!

ABOUT WHOM IS THIS SAID …?

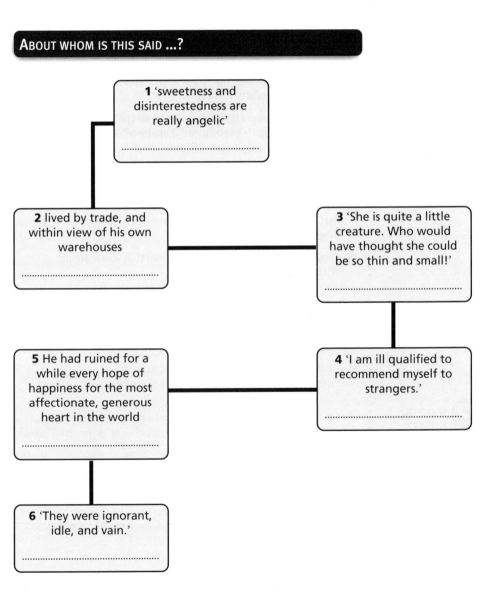

1 'sweetness and disinterestedness are really angelic'

....

2 lived by trade, and within view of his own warehouses

....

3 'She is quite a little creature. Who would have thought she could be so thin and small!'

....

5 He had ruined for a while every hope of happiness for the most affectionate, generous heart in the world

....

4 'I am ill qualified to recommend myself to strangers.'

....

6 'They were ignorant, idle, and vain.'

....

Check your answers on p. 113.

CHAPTERS 39–40 – The sisters are reunited

❶ On the journey home, the two sisters stop at a coaching inn where they are met by Kitty and Lydia.

❷ The younger sisters have squandered all their money shopping but Lydia is in such good spirits that she offers to treat them all to a meal so long as Jane and Elizabeth pay!

❸ Lydia tells her elders sisters that Wickham's regiment is about to move to Brighton.

❹ Back home, Elizabeth tells Jane of those parts of Darcy's letter that deal with Wickham but not about Darcy's influence with Bingley.

❺ They agree not to say anything of what they know about Wickham.

In the course of her ceaseless gossip about balls and officers, Lydia announces that Wickham's regiment is about to remove to Brighton. She has been begging her father to take them all down to Brighton for the summer. She also reveals that the affair between Wickham and Miss King is over. Knowing what she does, Elizabeth even sympathises with Lydia's rather tasteless remarks on the subject.

 DID YOU KNOW?

Lydia's cruel remark is a reminder of the reality that a genteel young woman's only hope of security was through marriage; becoming an old maid was a very real fear. In the last six years of her life Jane Austen's income from her novels amounted to only about £100 a year.

On the journey home Lydia tactlessly asks if Jane has been 'flirting' (Ch. 39, p. 181) in London because she risks being 'quite an old maid soon' at 'almost three and twenty' (Ch. 39, p. 181).

When they have arrived home, Elizabeth declines Lydia's invitation to walk into Meryton, largely because she dreads meeting Wickham again. She takes comfort that he will soon be moving on to Brighton, only to learn that her mother has been nagging Mr Bennet to agree to Lydia's scheme.

Jane finds it difficult to believe that Wickham could be so bad. Elizabeth cannot forgive herself for being so prejudiced towards Darcy, especially as she sees her dislike as stemming from pride in her own cleverness.

The two sisters agree not to broadcast the truth about Wickham, Jane because she fears it will do him harm, Elizabeth because it was given to her in confidence. Elizabeth detects a sadness about Jane and realises that her feelings for Bingley have not weakened. She finds little to say in response to her mother's persistent questioning.

> **CHECKPOINT 17**
>
> Why is it a mistake for Elizabeth and Jane to conceal the truth about Wickham?

> **Lydia**
>
> From this point, Lydia's 'animal spirits' (Ch. 9, p. 40) take on a new significance. Her giddy, irresponsible nature contrasts not only with Elizabeth's own character but seems to represent the worst of everything that Darcy may think of the Bennet family.

CHAPTERS 41–2 – Lydia ges her way

1 The regiment have a mere week remaining in Meryton. Lydia is invited to accompany Colonel Forster and his wife to Brighton.

2 Elizabeth attempts to persuade her father not to allow Lydia to go to Brighton.

3 Elizabeth meets Wickham and is ambiguous about how much she has learned of his past.

4 Lydia departs for Brighton and Elizabeth is left reflecting on her family's shortcomings.

5 Elizabeth goes to Derbyshire with the Gardiners.

 DID YOU KNOW?

Brighton was a fashionable resort made popular by the Prince Regent. It also had a reputation for immorality and corruption.

Elizabeth is acutely aware of the dangers in allowing Lydia to go to Brighton and appeals to her father to withhold his consent. She warns Mr Bennet that Lydia's behaviour has already brought the family into disrepute, Mr Bennet laughs off the suggestion. When Elizabeth presses him further by stressing Lydia's shallow and flirtatious nature, his response is that he finds it more convenient to grant Lydia's wishes, on the grounds that she can hardly become any worse, than to attempt to keep her under control.

Since she has returned to Longbourn, Elizabeth has been unable to avoid Wickham but now can see his charming manners in a different light: they now possess 'an affectation and a sameness to disgust and weary' (Ch. 41, p. 191). In their last conversation, Elizabeth is deliberately ambiguous about what she has learned from Colonel Fitzwilliam and Mr Darcy. Wickham's obvious discomfort makes it clear that he is worried that she knows the truth.

CHECKPOINT 18

How does Mr Bennet's reasons for marriage resemble Lydia's?

With Lydia's departure, Elizabeth is left to reflect on the deficiencies of her family and particularly on her father's weakness. 'Captivated by youth and beauty', he 'had married a woman whose weak understanding and illiberal mind, had very early in their marriage put an end to all real affection for her' (Ch. 42, p. 194). His response to this failure was not to turn to gambling or to drink but to retreat to his study from where he could regard his family with the eye of an amused observer. Elizabeth is now acutely aware that her father's detached and cynical outlook amounts to irresponsibility towards his children. Their uncontrolled behaviour threatens the family's good name.

Otherwise, she is bored and the tedium of life at Longbourn is only relieved by the prospect of the trip with the Gardiners. As the time approaches Mrs Gardiner writes to explain that the trip will have to be cut short so that they will not be able to journey further northwards than Derbyshire.

Once in Derbyshire, Elizabeth is at first reluctant to visit Pemberley for fear of meeting Darcy. However, reassured by the chambermaid at a local inn that the family are not in residence, her mind is put at ease.

Stuck at home

The chapters between Elizabeth's last encounter with Darcy in Kent and their next encounter in Derbyshire serve as an interlude. The fact that these emotionally significant events take place away from Longbourn emphasise the independence of Elizabeth's inner life. Her eventual move to become mistress of Pemberley reflects how she has outgrown the confines of Longbourn. It was Darcy who had earlier exclaimed '*You* cannot have been always at Longbourn' (Ch. 32, p. 149). These chapters focus on some of the worst aspects of life at Longbourn.

CHAPTER 43 – Pemberley impresses

❶ The party visits Pemberley.

❷ The housekeeper is full of praise for Darcy.

❸ Suddenly, Darcy appears. Elizabeth is covered in shame but Darcy is impeccably civil and even asks after her family.

❹ Darcy joins Elizabeth and the Gardiners on their walk and engages in friendly conversation.

❺ As Elizabeth listens to Darcy she is drawn to wonder whether he still loves her but she is still rather nervous of his presence.

❻ As they leave Elizabeth defends Darcy when Mrs Gardiner refers to his supposed treatment of Wickham.

 DID YOU KNOW?

It is likely that the fictional Pemberley is modelled on Chatsworth House in Derbyshire which it is believed Jane Austen visited in 1811.

Although Elizabeth is very nervous as they approach Pemberley she is 'delighted' (p. 201) at what she sees. Elizabeth and the Gardiners are shown around Pemberley by the housekeeper, an honest, plain-spoken woman who offers unqualified praise of Darcy's consideration and generosity. His reputation for being proud and aloof is simply owing to the fact that 'he does not rattle away like other young men' (p. 204). Elizabeth is astonished at this side to Darcy's character, which seems so much at odds with her own understanding.

GLOSSARY

affectation manner

illiberal narrow-minded

As Elizabeth and the Gardiners walk away from the house, Darcy suddenly appears; he has returned unexpectedly early. Shame and distress overcome Elizabeth as she cannot bear to think what Darcy will make of her presence at his home. To her amazement, Darcy conducts himself with impeccable civility and even enquires warmly about her family. After he has left, Elizabeth begins to regain her composure but her thoughts are constantly on Darcy and what he must be feeling about her.

Before long, Darcy reappears and joins them on their walk. He engages Mr and Mrs Gardiner in amiable conversation and Elizabeth takes pleasure in the fact that she has some relations of whom she need not feel ashamed. She is informed that Bingley and his sisters are due the next day but she is particularly intrigued and flattered when Darcy tells her that his sister wants to meet her.

DID YOU KNOW?

The housekeeper who shows Elizabeth and the Gardiners the family portraits is Mrs Reynolds, who shares her name with a famous portrait painter. A joke?

As they leave Pemberley, Mr and Mrs Gardiner, who know him only by reputation, try to weigh up Darcy's character. When Mrs Gardiner dwells on his supposed treatment of Wickham, Elizabeth rushes to Darcy's defence.

Darcy in his natural environment

The visit to Pemberley is crucial within the narrative scheme of the novel as, for the first time, we see Darcy relaxed and wholly at ease on his home ground. This previously unsuspected face of Darcy impresses the Gardiners and affects Elizabeth deeply.

There are subtler dimensions to the visit as well. It is not only Darcy's behaviour that moves Elizabeth but the *place* as well. She later confides to Jane that she first felt she loved Darcy when she saw 'his beautiful grounds at Pemberley' (Ch. 59, p. 301). Jane Austen's description of the grounds stresses the effortless blend of art and nature: 'She had never seen a place for which nature had done more, or where natural beauty had been so little counteracted by an awkward taste' (p. 201). The grounds, which are ten miles round, represent great power and wealth, but Elizabeth is impressed by the evidence of natural *taste*, so different from Lady Catherine's vulgarity.

CHAPTER 44 – Elizabeth's hopes rise

1 Darcy brings his sister to meet Elizabeth.

2 Bingley arrives and Elizabeth sees that he is still in love with Jane.

3 All are invited to dine at Pemberley.

4 When Elizabeth is alone she is overcome with a sense of gratitude towards Darcy and she feels 'a real interest in his welfare' (p. 216).

It turns out that the 'proud' (p. 212) Georgiana is merely extremely shy and Elizabeth is relieved that she is simply a pleasant, unassuming young woman.

Bingley soon arrives and Elizabeth poses herself the problem of guessing the true feelings of her visitors. She satisfies herself that Bingley shows no attachment to Miss Darcy and when he recalls the precise date he last saw Jane, she is gratified that his affection for her sister is undimmed. As for Darcy, his manner is wholly different from that she had witnessed at Netherfield and Rosings.

An invitation is extended to dine at Pemberley and when the visitors leave, Elizabeth hastens away to be alone. Her feelings towards Darcy have undergone a decisive change. She dismisses any thoughts of hatred. They have been supplanted by a warm sense of gratitude, respect and concern for his wellbeing. Nevertheless, she is nervous about thoughts of marriage.

DID YOU KNOW?

The 'beautiful pyramids of grapes, nectarines, and peaches' (Ch. 45, p. 219) which were on the table would have been specially grown in the greenhouses at Pemberley. There were no supermarkets in Jane Austen's day!

CHAPTER 45 – Miss Bingley is put down

1 Elizabeth and the Gardiners visit Pemberley, where the party includes the Bingley sisters.

2 Miss Bingley shows her jealousy of Elizabeth.

The atmosphere is strained at first and is only eased by the cordial conversation of Mrs Gardiner and Miss Darcy's companion, Mrs Annesley. Miss Bingley cannot resist showing her jealousy of Elizabeth by making a thinly disguised reference to Wickham. Elizabeth feels for the embarrassment that Darcy and his sister must be feeling.

DID YOU KNOW?

In Jane Austen's day 'handsome' could be used to describe women as well as men. When used of a woman, 'handsome' conveyed a kind of dignified or elegant beauty beyond mere glamour or prettiness.

When Elizabeth and the Gardeners have left, Miss Bingley sets about criticising Elizabeth's appearance until Darcy's composure snaps and he leaves the room praising Elizabeth as one of the 'handsomest women of my acquaintance' (p. 221).

Boiling passions

Miss Bingley shows her desperation by openly criticising Elizabeth in the crudest of terms. Her tactless remarks contrast with the civility of the Gardiners, whom she would regard her social inferiors. Previously, Darcy had dismissed Caroline's attacks with deadpan **irony**. His uncharacteristic outburst is a measure of the passions that are boiling beneath the surface.

CHAPTERS 46–8 – Catastrophe!

❶ Elizabeth's world collapses when she receives two letters from Jane with the news that Lydia has eloped with Wickham and, as far as is known, they are not married.

❷ Darcy enters and is plainly alarmed and concerned for her.

❸ Darcy leaves promising not to reveal anything about what has happened while Elizabeth and the Gardiners set off for Longbourn.

❹ On her return Elizabeth finds an hysterical mother and learns that Mr Bennet has gone to London in search of the couple.

❺ Colonel Foster arrives with a letter Lydia has written to his wife in which she teats the affair as a huge joke.

❻ Eventually Mr Bennet gives up the search and returns home.

Trembling from the shock at the news of the elopement, Elizabeth's first thought is to seek her uncle, but at that moment Darcy enters. In her shame and despair, Elizabeth realises that she could love Darcy, but the chance is now lost forever. The dinner at Pemberley is cancelled and Darcy leaves readily promising not to reveal anything of what has happened. Elizabeth and the Gardiners immediately depart for Longbourn.

On the journey back to Longbourn, Mr Gardiner tries to evaluate the seriousness of the situation. Elizabeth doubts whether Wickham has any intention of marrying Lydia. She candidly lays much of the blame on her father whom she thinks has made no attempt to correct Lydia's waywardness, although when the regiment were at Meryton there were no signs of any particular familiarity between Wickham and her sister.

On their arrival, Jane is unable to add any further news. Mr Bennet is in London attempting to trace the couple but so far there has been no word. Mrs Bennet is hysterical and blames everyone but herself. When Mr Gardiner proposes returning to London to assist his brother-in-law, she can think of nothing but Lydia's wedding clothes and being bereaved and homeless when Wickham kills her husband. Mrs Bennet's indiscriminate talk of Mr Bennet's murder and Lydia's

DID YOU KNOW?
The population of London had reached one million by Jane Austen's day and although then, as now, it was the hub of cultural and social life, it was also regarded as a dangerous place.

wedding dress in the same breath, is wildly comic but emphasises her moral bankruptcy. Mary has some bookish reflections, whilst Kitty is somewhat sobered by the fact that she, in fact, had known of Lydia's attachment for some time.

Colonel Foster has visited, bearing a letter Lydia had sent his wife. In it Lydia treats the whole affair as a delightful joke and fully expects that she and Wickham will be married. Despite her criticisms, Elizabeth feels for her father and despairs of maintaining any vestiges of the family reputation.

CHECKPOINT 19

What does her letter tell us about Lydia?

Longbourn is plunged into a state of hopelessness. The expected letter from Mr Bennet is not forthcoming and a flood of local stories about Wickham's evil ways only serves to emphasise the misery. Mr Collins's letter of condolence simply expresses his condemnation of the family and his relief at not having married into it. Eventually, Mr Bennet gives up his search and returns home dispirited and acknowledging his own guilt in the affair. However, he still cannot resist teasing Kitty by declaring that he will be very severe on her in the future.

The big divide

After the harmony of Pemberley with its reassuring sense of wellbeing, Lydia's elopement strikes a sharply discordant note. It also emphasises the gulf between the two moral orders of Pemberley and Longbourn, a divide which Elizabeth now despairs of ever crossing. She is more conscious than ever of her family's inadequacies and is quite frank about their failings and candidly lays much of the blame on her father's irresponsibility.

CHAPTERS 49–50 – Salvation!

❶ Mr Gardiner writes to say the couple have been found and Wickham has agreed to a modest settlement.

❷ Overjoyed, Mrs Bennet makes extravagant plans for the impending wedding.

❸ **Elizabeth regrets telling Darcy of the affair and fears she has lost him forever.**

❹ **Mr Gardiner writes to confirm that Wickham has accepted the deal.**

When Mr Bennet learns of the settlement, he suspects that his brother-in-law has paid Wickham a very much larger sum than he claims to induce him to marry Lydia and Mr Bennet does not know how he can pay him back.

Mrs Bennet is naturally overjoyed when she learns of her daughter's impending marriage and her thoughts immediately turn to clothes. She dismisses any generosity on her brother's part as no more than is due to them. Elizabeth is not hopeful of Lydia's chances of happiness but accepts that the situation could have been much worse.

Mr Bennet is troubled by the burden of indebtedness to his brother-in-law but is relieved that his immediate expenses will be slight. We learn that he has been financially imprudent in the past and made no provision for the eventuality of having no male heir. Mrs Bennet makes extravagant plans for the newlyweds to settle locally in a fine house, but she is outraged when Mr Bennet refuses even to spend any money on Lydia. To her, such neglect is worse than the shame of her daughter's behaviour.

Elizabeth's thoughts turn to Darcy. She regrets that she has told him of Lydia's actions, although she doubts whether Darcy would want to be associated with her family under any circumstances. She has come to understand what it is to be Darcy and appreciate his generous spirit. She longs that the clock could be turned back, for now he is lost to her, she knows that she loves him.

Mr Gardiner writes with the latest news that Wickham has accepted an 'ensigncy' (Ch. 50, p. 252) in the north of England and that his debts are in the process of being discharged. Mr Bennet backs down on his decision never to allow Lydia and Wickham to enter Longbourn.

DID YOU KNOW?

Until the nineteenth century, brides generally married in their favourite dress rather than a special wedding dress.

DID YOU KNOW?

The post of an ensign was the lowest grade of commissioned officer in an infantry regiment.

DID YOU KNOW?

Elopements are often seen as romantic, but if Darcy had not arranged their marriage Lydia would have been ruined and become a social outcast, whilst Wickham was still thinking of 'making his fortune by marriage' (Ch. 52, p. 260).

Balancing act

In some respects Chapters 49–50 balance Chapters 46–8. The situation changes from one of utter despair to one that offers some hope, highlighting Mrs Bennet's violent change of mood but also in Elizabeth's relief that the situation could be much worse.

Now take a break!

Who says ... About whom?

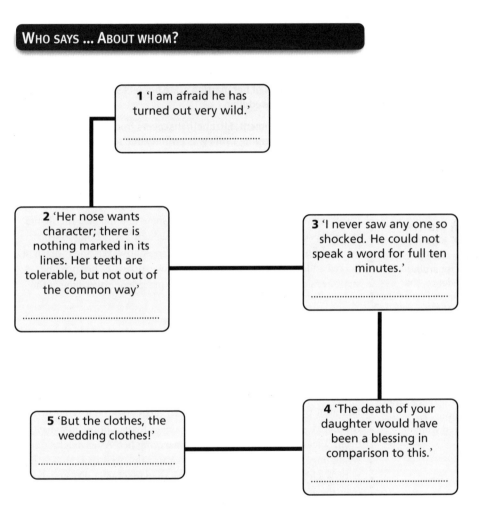

1 'I am afraid he has turned out very wild.'

....

2 'Her nose wants character; there is nothing marked in its lines. Her teeth are tolerable, but not out of the common way'

....

3 'I never saw any one so shocked. He could not speak a word for full ten minutes.'

....

4 'The death of your daughter would have been a blessing in comparison to this.'

....

5 'But the clothes, the wedding clothes!'

....

Check your answers on p. 113.

CHAPTERS 51–2 – An amazing revelation

❶ The newlyweds arrive at Longbourn. To Elizabeth's disgust, Lydia vulgarly boasts of her married state but lets slip that Darcy was present at the wedding.

❷ To her astonishment, Elizabeth discovers from Mrs Gardiner that Wickham's marrying Lydia was entirely due to Mr Darcy's intervention.

❸ Elizabeth and Wickham meet; without actually saying so she makes it clear that she knows the truth about his past.

DID YOU KNOW?

There were involved rules regarding precedence, that is who goes first or is given the most favourable position at a public gathering, for instance. Lydia is correct in claiming precedence over her eldest sister because she is now a married woman.

Elizabeth tries to put herself in Lydia's shoes and imagine the shame and embarrassment she would feel. Lydia's arrival at Longbourn after her wedding is attended by no such feelings, however. She is brash and brazen and, far from showing any remorse, boasts of her married state, even declaring that she now takes precedence over Jane at the dinner table.

Elizabeth's disgust at Lydia's vulgarity is soon displaced by her astonishment when her sister lets slip that Darcy was present at her wedding. Consumed with curiosity, she writes to Mrs Gardiner enquiring after the truth.

Her aunt writes back that it was, in fact, Darcy who tracked down the couple. He soon discovered that, whatever Lydia's hopes may have been, Wickham had no intention of marrying her. After much wrangling, Darcy succeeded in coming to a financial accommodation with Wickham, so that he would agree to marry Lydia. Darcy talked over the arrangements with Mr Gardiner but refused to allow him to make any contribution. However, in order to conceal his role in the affair, Darcy persuaded Mr Gardiner to take the credit for the settlement.

Elizabeth finds herself astonished on Darcy's behalf; she knows what it must have taken to have gone to such lengths to help a woman 'whom he must abominate and despise' and a man 'whom he always most wished to avoid' (Ch. 52, p. 263). For a fleeting moment, Elizabeth dares to think that he might have done all this for her. Her thoughts are interrupted by Wickham who once again attempts to find out how much she knows of his past. This time, Elizabeth is less guarded and her pointed replies leave Wickham in little doubt that his deceit has been exposed. Even so, seemingly unable to feel or express any remorse, Wickham kisses Elizabeth's hand as though they are the best of friends. Out of a sense of responsibility, if not respect, towards her youngest sister, Elizabeth treats Wickham with good humour. Her skilful management of their last conversation enables her to draw a veil over his past behaviour, while making it abundantly clear that she is fully acquainted with his nature.

Plot development

From a narrative **point of view** the elopement is a device to force Darcy and Elizabeth apart and then to throw them together again. In purely realistic terms, it would have been perfectly feasible for Darcy to have proposed at Pemberley but that would have led to rather a limp ending. The novel needs a dramatic **denouement**, a sense of danger and threat averted before the final celebrations.

CHAPTERS 53–5 – Jane is happy at last

1 Wickham and Lydia leave for Newcastle and Bingley is rumoured to be returning to Netherfield.

2 Before long Bingley visits the Bennets accompanied by Darcy.

3 Elizabeth is terrified of facing Darcy after all that has happened but is pleased that Bingley is attentive to Jane.

4 On their next visit Bingley shows increasing affection towards Jane but Darcy is very distant and soon departs for London.

5 To everyone's joy, Bingley proposes at last.

At first Mrs Bennet expresses total indifference to the thought of Bingley's return but, before long, she is anxious to be the first to invite him to dinner. Jane plainly still feels for Bingley and is disturbed by the prospect of seeing him again, despite her assurances to the

? DID YOU KNOW?

In the pre-railway age, Newcastle would have seemed very remote – even to one such as Darcy, who thought nothing of travelling 50 miles a day.

GLOSSARY
abominate loathe

contrary. Having seen him at Pemberley, Elizabeth is reasonably convinced that Bingley is still drawn to her sister but she is uncertain that he is a free agent in the matter. Soon after his arrival, Bingley presents himself at Longbourn accompanied, to everyone's surprise, by Mr Darcy.

CHECKPOINT 20

In what way is Mrs Bennet particularly rude to Darcy?

Torn between hope and terror, Elizabeth buries herself in her needlework, hardly daring to look up. Jane is no less uneasy. Darcy seems less at ease than he had been in Derbyshire and barely speaks but he endures Mrs Bennet's extreme rudeness with composure.

Elizabeth is once again covered in shame at her mother's behaviour but is heartened as Bingley becomes increasingly attentive to Jane.

After the gentlemen have left, Elizabeth is left pondering Darcy's motives in making the visit and decides to give him no further thought, whilst Jane declares that she can now treat Bingley merely as an acquaintance. The next time the two gentlemen visit, Bingley shows his continuing attachment to Jane but Elizabeth, who has been building her hopes on Darcy's showing some clear sign of his continuing interest in her, is disappointed. He seems strangely distant and they exchange scarcely more than a few passing words. Darcy's apparent avoidance of Elizabeth shows his underlying shyness and how nervous he is that he should be rejected once again. Elizabeth cannot believe that Darcy can still love her. However, Elizabeth becomes almost cross with Jane for refusing to recognise Bingley's affection.

CHECKPOINT 21

In what ways would Elizabeth now be likely to feel more sympathetic towards Charlotte than before?

Darcy leaves for London but is due to return in ten days. Meanwhile, Bingley becomes a regular visitor and Mrs Bennet is so encouraged by his attentiveness that she contrives to leave him alone with Jane. At first, her comic subterfuge is not rewarded: the hoped-for proposal is not forthcoming. Before long, however, Jane declares her happiness. Elizabeth wryly reflects on how all the attempts to frustrate this relationship have finally come to nought. She is delighted for Jane, confident in the belief that Bingley's affection is 'rationally founded' (Ch. 55, p. 280) and that the couple are ideally matched.

Jane's joy is tempered slightly by her concern for Elizabeth's future happiness. Elizabeth, with characteristic resilience and good humour, reassures her sister that a second Mr Collins may yet appear.

CHAPTERS 56–7 – Lady Catherine meets her match

1 Lady Catherine arrives at Longbourn demanding to talk to Elizabeth.

2 Lady Catherine, having been informed that Darcy and Elizabeth intend to marry, demands that Elizabeth denies the reports.

3 Elizabeth is incensed by Lady Catherine's arrogance and refuses to do anything of the sort. She asks Lady Catherine to leave.

4 A letter arrives from Mr Collins condemning the 'evils' (Ch. 57, p. 292) of the betrothal of Darcy and Elizabeth.

Events take a surprising turn with the sudden and unannounced arrival of Lady Catherine at the gates of Longbourn. She sweeps in and, after some disparaging remarks about the house and gardens, demands an interview with Elizabeth. As they make their way to a private corner of the garden, Elizabeth wonders how she could possibly have imagined that this arrogant, overbearing woman was at all like Darcy. It turns out that Lady Catherine has been informed that Darcy and Elizabeth intend to marry and she has come to demand that Elizabeth denies the report, although she is convinced it must be false. Elizabeth refuses to be browbeaten by Lady Catherine and responds to her attempts at intimidation with composure. The emptiness of Lady Catherine's accusations and threats are exposed and countered with characteristic alertness and skill.

Elizabeth is clearly incensed by Lady Catherine's arrogance but maintains her dignity in the face of an onslaught on her character and breeding. Eventually, however, Elizabeth declares that she will be insulted no longer and brings the interview to a close. To Elizabeth's relief, her mother believes that the 'very fine-looking' (Ch. 56, p. 289) woman was merely making a courtesy call.

CHECKPOINT 22

What do we learn about Elizabeth's feelings towards her family during the confrontation with Lady Catherine?

DID YOU KNOW?

It would have been seen as the height of rudeness to arrive uninvited and unintroduced like Lady Catherine. Remember Mr Bennett pays a *formal* visit to introduce himself to Mr Bingley.

Elizabeth is left to speculate on the extraordinary visit. Despite her strong-willed resistance to Lady Catherine's threats and demands, she is disturbed by the encounter. She guesses that the rumour of her engagement to Darcy had begun with the Lucases and reached Lady Catherine via Charlotte and Mr Collins. She is less certain about Darcy's response to pressure from his aunt. She fears that he may well be swayed by arguments concerning his loss of status and dignity.

Mr Bennet shows Elizabeth a letter he has just received from Mr Collins warning of the 'evils' (Ch. 57, p. 292) which will follow from the anticipated betrothal of Darcy and Elizabeth. He is highly amused by the notion of Elizabeth being in any way attracted to a man who has probably never looked at her in his life and invites his daughter to share in his hilarity. Elizabeth responds politely, but when her father stumbles on the truth by asking whether Lady Catherine had called to withhold her consent, she feels hurt and isolated, since no one can even suspect her true feelings.

A clash of cultures

Lady Catherine's dramatic intervention does, of course, **ironically** precipitate the very marriage she is attempting to avert. The confrontation can also be viewed as a clash of the old order and the new. Lady Catherine, steeped in her aristocratic past, can only threaten and talk angrily about honour, decorum and prudence. Elizabeth, however, is coolly rational, skilfully demolishing each of Lady Catherine's charges in turn. Elizabeth takes command by virtue of her integrity and the scope of her intelligence. She is well aware of the shortcomings of the Bennets but she will not allow them to be criticised by one such as Lady Catherine.

CHAPTERS 58–9 – Breaking the ice

1 Elizabeth fully expects not to see Darcy again but Bingley brings him to Longbourn.

2 As they are out walking, Elizabeth decides to confront Darcy with the issue of his intervention in the affair of Wickham and Lydia.

3 Darcy confesses he did everything for Elizabeth's sake and his love is undimmed. He proposes and is accepted.

4 The couple now delight in tracing the history of their turbulent relationship and how they came to realise they loved each other.

5 The Bennet family are astonished that Elizabeth is to marry the man of whom she had expressed such fierce dislike.

 DID YOU KNOW?

Rather like balls, walks offered young men and women an opportunity for more intimate conversation than was normally possible in formal situations.

Elizabeth, considering Lady Catherine's influence with her nephew, rather expects Darcy to send his apologies and fail to return as promised but her hopes revive when, before long, Bingley brings him to Longbourn. The party set off on a walk and Elizabeth finds herself alone in Darcy's company. Unable to stand the tension any longer, she takes the initiative and broaches the subject of his intervention in the affair of Wickham and Lydia. As though relieved of a burden by being able to share the truth, he explains that his actions were entirely for

DID YOU KNOW?

The 'walk' was something of a social activity in Jane Austen's day and rather like the ball or the musical evening. The very rich incorporated walks into the design of their estates.

her sake and that his love is undimmed. They walk on, gradually unfolding the development of their feelings towards one another. Ironically, what finally brought them together was Lady Catherine's attempt to force them apart. When she told Darcy of Elizabeth's stubborn refusal to give in to her demands, he dared hope once again that his feelings were not in vain.

Together, they explore the twists and turns of their relationship. Darcy admits that he had been stung by Elizabeth's justified accusation that he had behaved in an ungentlemanly manner (Ch. 34). For her part, she confesses her wilful and headstrong character had blinded her to the truth. It emerges that Darcy has not only endorsed Bingley's attachment to Jane but apologises for and agrees that his previous interference was 'impertinent' (Ch. 58, p. 298).

By the end of the walk, the couple's previous differences have melted away but Elizabeth restrains herself from making a joke at Darcy's expense, remembering that he has yet to learn how to be teased.

The skies may have cleared for Elizabeth but she is still left with the question of how to inform her unsuspecting family. Even Jane, who is the first to be informed, reacts in astonishment and disbelief, so convinced was she of Elizabeth's thorough dislike of Darcy. Elizabeth explains that she could not discuss her confused feelings for Darcy without having to mention Bingley. Jane clears Elizabeth of the charge of slyness and the two sisters talk well into the night.

The next morning, to Mrs Bennet's expressed disgust, Darcy reappears. The couple agree that the parents' permission to marry should be sought without delay. On hearing the news, Mr Bennet is shocked and anxious that his daughter has not made a dreadful mistake. Elizabeth reassures her father who frankly admits that, in any case, he has already given his consent because he is too overawed by Mr Darcy to refuse him anything. When Elizabeth speaks to her mother she is, for once, speechless but the thought of ten thousand pounds a year soon dispels her professed dislike of Darcy.

> **CHECKPOINT 23**
>
> Why is Mrs Bennet's reaction to the engagement of Darcy and Elizabeth amusingly ironic?

Resolution

The return of Darcy, encouraged by what he has heard from his aunt about Elizabeth's defiance, signals the final passage of the novel towards its resolution but not without some minor ripples of comic suspense. Elizabeth was exasperated at Jane's indifference to Bingley's obvious admiration and despite repeated visits and Mrs Bennet's contrivance, it seemed that he would never propose. For her part, hope and fear transform her into a coy, blushing young woman, while Darcy becomes an awkward tongue-tied suitor.

CHAPTERS 60–1 – All's well

1. Elizabeth learns more from Darcy about how his love for her developed.

2. Letters of congratulation arrive.

3. Jane and Elizabeth are married on the same day.

4. Bingley and Jane move to Derbyshire within easy reach of Darcy and Elizabeth at Pemberley, to which Mr Bennet becomes a frequent visitor.

> **GLOSSARY**
> **impertinent** out of place, rude

Now that everything is settled, Elizabeth begins to enjoy her new situation and quizzes Darcy on the progress of his love for her. This offers a useful comment on the novel's events. She learns that he admired her for the liveliness of her mind and that the reason for his reticence on his recent visits to Longbourn was simply embarrassment. She admits to the same sensation and they rejoice in recalling how the ice was finally broken.

There follows an exchange of letters:

● Elizabeth writes to Mrs Gardiner expressing her unconfined joy

● Mr Bennet writes a short letter to Mr Collins confirming the engagement, advising him that his interests lie with Mr Darcy rather than Lady Catherine

● Miss Bingley sends her congratulations but her insincerity is clear even to Jane

● By contrast, Miss Darcy writes warmly, expressing genuine delight

Before long Mr Collins and Charlotte come to stay at Lucas Lodge, the latter relieved to escape Lady Catherine's ill temper. Darcy manages to withstand Mr Collins's excessive flattery and Sir William's extravagant compliments but Elizabeth finds it necessary to protect him from Mrs Philips's vulgarity. The removal to Pemberley is looked forward to as a relief from such unwelcome attentions.

Mrs Bennet who, despite having her wildest dreams fulfilled, remains as silly as ever but the lives of all members of the families are altered in some way by the marriages:

● Bingley and Jane feel obliged to escape Mrs Bennet's attentions by moving to Derbyshire, happily within easy reach of Pemberley.

● Mr Bennet misses Elizabeth deeply but compensates with frequent visits to Pemberley.

● Free of Lydia's influence, Kitty becomes much more sensible.

● Mary breaks out of her shell and becomes more sociable.

 DID YOU KNOW?

Some people are never satisfied. At least a dozen sequels to *Pride and Prejudice* were published in the twentieth century, including two by Emma Tennant: *Pemberley or Pride and Prejudice continued* (1993) and *An Unequal Marriage: or Pride and Prejudice Twenty Years Later* (1994).

- Lydia is still incorrigible and writes to Elizabeth demanding that Darcy should provide them with additional income. She and Wickham are constantly in debt and their relationship is distinctly cooling.

- Miss Bingley prefers to make her peace with Elizabeth than to be excluded from Pemberley.

- Georgiana and Elizabeth become very close, though Georgiana never fails to wonder at Elizabeth's playful manner with her brother.

- Lady Catherine's anger is eventually supplanted by curiosity and she deigns to descend on Pemberley.

- Elizabeth's and Darcy's indebtedness to the Gardiners is reflected in their enduring closeness and affection.

A quiet revolution?

The final chapter is a kind of mirror of a society which has achieved a state of relative equilibrium and stability. In effect, a quiet revolution has taken place: old prejudices have been banished by the formation of new alliances. The world may be an imperfect place and some things cannot be improved. Neither Mrs Bennet nor Lady Catherine will achieve true gentility and Lydia and Wickham will continue to pursue their flimsy dreams but Pemberley appears to offer a glimpse of an ideal world.

A constant thread that ran through the work of the eighteenth-century writers Jane Austen so admired was the pursuit of happiness and it may not be too fanciful to suggest that *Pride and Prejudice* celebrates that ideal. She was no revolutionary, but it is curious to note that the famous opening sentence offers a faint, if **ironic**, echo of the Declaration of American Independence: 'We hold these truths to be self-evident, that all men … are endowed by their Creator with certain unalienable Rights, that among these are Life, Liberty and the pursuit of Happiness.'

DID YOU KNOW?

The French Revolution entered Jane Austen's life when the husband of her cousin, Eliza, was guillotined in 1794.

Now take a break!

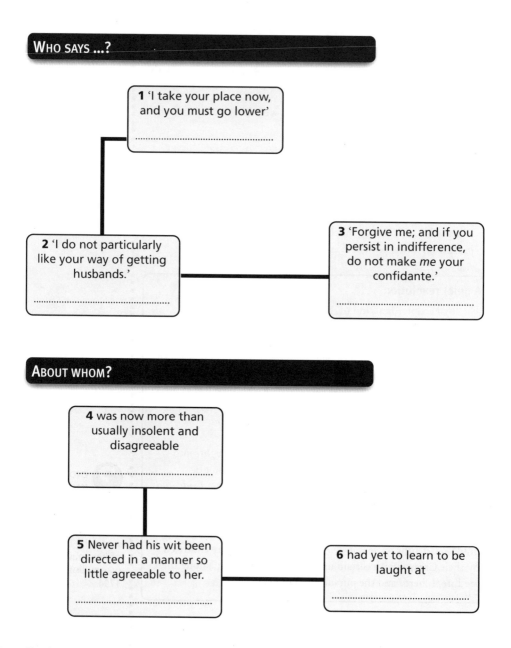

Who says ...?

1 'I take your place now, and you must go lower'

....

2 'I do not particularly like your way of getting husbands.'

....

3 'Forgive me; and if you persist in indifference, do not make *me* your confidante.'

....

About whom?

4 was now more than usually insolent and disagreeable

....

5 Never had his wit been directed in a manner so little agreeable to her.

....

6 had yet to learn to be laught at

....

Check your answers on p. 113.

PART THREE

COMMENTARY

THEMES

To reduce a novel by Jane Austen to a set of themes is necessarily to oversimplify and to abuse that 'delicacy' which her early admirer, Sir Walter Scott, so appreciated. Nevertheless, there are concerns or areas of interest that permeate her work. They are, however, subtly intertwined so that it is difficult to approach the novel from one **point of view** without impinging on another viewpoint. The central focus is, of course, Elizabeth, and her 'character' is inseparable from the consideration of almost any aspect of the work.

LOVE AND MARRIAGE

At face value, *Pride and Prejudice* is a **romantic** comedy and Jane Austen acknowledges how romantic feelings may overwhelm us. For couples in love, their joy can never be understated; their world is complete or, as one poet (John Donne) put it, 'nothing else is'. Few are immune. Lydia will never be happy without her 'angel' (Ch. 47, p. 236), Wickham. Jane feels she is 'the happiest creature in the world' (Ch. 55, p. 279), whilst Elizabeth declares she is 'happier even than Jane' (Ch. 59, p. 300).

But whilst romantic passion needs to be celebrated, it offers an incomplete picture of human relationships. Jane Austen makes it clear that the passion of the moment is a poor foundation for lasting happiness. Mr Bennet had been 'captivated by youth and beauty' (Ch. 42, p. 194) but Mrs Bennet's 'weak understanding and illiberal mind' (Ch. 42, p. 194) prevented any lasting affection. By the end of the novel Lydia's and Wickham's reckless relationship has already descended into an existence which is 'unsettled in the extreme' (Ch. 61, p. 311). Their marriage will not even be supported by the relative financial and social status that Mr and Mrs Bennet are able to enjoy.

Charlotte by contrast is wholly unsentimental: 'I am not a romantic ... I ask only a comfortable home' (Ch. 22, p. 105). Her readiness to settle for financial security to the exclusion of all other considerations, which

DID YOU KNOW?
The romantic novel, as we know it today, was relatively new in Jane Austen's day and was not always approved of. Often young ladies had to read them in secret!

GLOSSARY
illiberal narrow-minded

so disturbs Elizabeth, is also not a basis for a true marriage. Ironically, like Mr Bennet, who retreats to his study, Charlotte soon learns to cope by using a back room so as to keep out of her husband's way.

DID YOU KNOW?

The word 'rational' when applied to human relationships, didn't mean calculated but the opposite of foolish or extravagant.

If such marriages signify discord, the ideal relationship should signify harmony. Elizabeth approves of Jane and Bingley for just this reason; their happiness is not simply based on physical attraction but is 'rationally founded' (Ch. 55, p. 280) and the couple possess a 'general similarity of feeling and taste' (Ch. 55, p. 280). Likewise, Mr Gardiner's 'sensible, gentlemanlike' character is complemented by his wife's 'amiable, intelligent' (Ch. 25, p. 118) personality.

The marriage of Elizabeth and Darcy, however, represents a much more complex state of affairs. Jane and Bingley's marriage is prudent on the basis of shared temperament and taste. Despite setbacks their feelings for each other do not change. By contrast, Elizabeth and Darcy achieve mutual admiration and respect only through the painful process of stripping away misunderstanding and self-deception, as they reveal to each other in Chapter 58. Their marriage is rational because they have learned to know *why* they love each other and it is secure because it is hard won (see also **Setting and background** and **Characters**).

THE ROLE OF WOMEN

In the conventional society of Jane Austen's day, a woman's role was fairly clear. Put most crudely, her position in life was defined by her father or her husband and she was expected to be modest, submissive and incapable of independent thought. With few exceptions, their education was inferior to that of their male contemporaries. Jane Austen was, of course, part of that society and in many respects the very form and subject of her novels would seem to accept women's traditional role. She is not, however, uncritical. Ignorance is certainly not bliss in Jane Austen's world; moral deficiency is closely linked with a narrowness of outlook, often compounded by lack of intelligence. It is easy to laugh at Mrs Bennet's 'fidgets' (Ch. 53, p. 267) and her wild changes of mood but she remains a 'woman of mean understanding' (Ch. 1, p. 7) who is incapable of exercising any moral discrimination. Lydia's 'animal spirits' (Ch. 9, p. 40) are likewise linked to the fact that she is 'vain, ignorant, idle' (Ch. 41, p. 190). The

simpering Caroline Bingley and the overbearing Lady Catherine also
reveal their cultural poverty when they display their lack of genuine
interest in reading and music. The comfortable Charlotte does not
lack intelligence but she sacrifices her individuality by marrying
Mr Collins.

Much of this ignorance we see through Elizabeth's eyes. She cannot
abide small talk – 'Their table was superlatively stupid. Scarcely a
syllable was uttered that did not relate to the game' (Ch. 29, p. 139) –
preferring the greater stimulus of conversational fencing with the
gentlemen. The characterisation of Elizabeth seems to represent
something of a departure from the conventional image of women at that
time. Above all, she possesses **wit**, intelligence and an independence of
thought that sets her apart, even from her elder sister. It has been argued
that the picture we have of Elizabeth reflects the views of thinkers such
as Mary Wollstonecraft, whose pioneering writing on women's rights
argued that in order to aspire to equality, women should devote their
energies to reason and independent thought.

However, it would be wrong to suggest that Elizabeth entirely
represents 'new woman'. Despite her misgivings, she is a dutiful
daughter and whilst she was prepared to reject one of the richest men
in England, ultimately she is anxious to assume her role as mistress of
Pemberley: 'she looked forward with delight to the time when they
should be removed from society so little pleasing to either, to all the
comfort and elegance of their family party at Pemberley' (Ch. 60, p.
309).

SOCIAL AND MORAL PERSPECTIVE

The distinction between gentry and trade is closely interwoven into
the novel's social relationships:

- Darcy prides himself on being a gentleman with all the duties and
  obligations that his status entails. And, as Caroline Bingley
  constantly reminds him, he would be lowering himself by
  associating with the Bennet family as they are connected with trade.

- Elizabeth, however, strongly asserts her dignity when she tells
  Lady Catherine: 'He [Darcy] is a gentleman; I am a gentleman's
  daughter; so far we are equal' (Ch. 56, p. 287).

**? DID YOU
KNOW?**
Mary Wollstonecraft
(1759–97) was
mother of Mary
Shelley, author of
'Frankenstein'.

- Conversely, the high-minded Miss Bingley forgets that the source of the family fortune, on which their status is founded, is trade. Sir William Lucas's background is also in trade but he devotes all his energies in proving his credentials to be a country gentleman.

- By contrast, Mr and Mrs Gardiner make no apologies for their participation in trade yet display a true gentility that impresses Mr Darcy.

- Lady Catherine, however, displays a vulgarity wholly unworthy of her social position.

DID YOU KNOW?

Mary Wollstonecraft wrote *A Vindication of the Rights of Woman* (1792) in which she complained: 'It would be an endless task to trace the variety of meannesses, cares and sorrows, into which women are plunged by the prevailing opinion that they were created rather to feel than reason ...'.

Throughout *Pride and Prejudice*, Jane Austen sets moral status against social status. Much of Elizabeth's initial dislike of Darcy can be seen as revulsion that, in his supposed treatment of Wickham, his moral standards are not worthy of his standing in society. The corollary is that Darcy, whilst 'bewitched' (Ch. 10, p. 46) by Elizabeth, cannot rid himself of thoughts of her social inferiority.

Charlotte seeks a comfortable compromise but although she acquires the social advantage of being a clergyman's wife she 'sacrificed every better feeling' (Ch. 22, p. 105). While Georgiana possesses the social advantage, her shy, unassuming demeanour belies her status and wealth. Mr Collins may seem to be no more than a figure of fun but his absurdity may also expose the dangers of social respectability without social and moral responsibility. In gaining a position in the Church, he has succeeded where Wickham failed, but for all the outward differences in their personalities, they both put self-interest before concern for others

It is interesting to observe that the plot's resolution is brought about by moral alliances that cross class boundaries. The gentleman, Darcy, conspires with the tradesman, Mr Gardiner, to rescue Lydia and the Bennets from social disgrace. Some may object that Elizabeth enjoys the best of two worlds; she has the pleasure of rejecting Darcy and the pleasure of accepting him. Her conversion to the material joys of Pemberley seems inconsistent with her criticisms of Charlotte's preoccupation with financial security. Such a change of heart is demanded by the conventions of the **romantic** novel, but in Jane Austen's scheme of things, the marriage of Elizabeth and Darcy may also represent an enrichment and rejuvenation of the traditional social order. Elizabeth's assertiveness is redirected so as to invest Pemberley, and all that it stands for, with a new sense of purpose (see also **Setting and background**).

PRIDE AND PREJUDICE

It is not difficult to find *examples* of these characteristics:

● Darcy is excessively proud of his social standing and his sense of superiority engenders a prejudiced view of Elizabeth and her kind.

● Conversely Elizabeth and the neighbourhood take against Darcy from the outset. Whether this prejudice stems from hurt pride or small-town suspicion of those with power and influence, it seriously colours Elizabeth's judgement.

● Exaggerated pride is perhaps displayed most clearly by Lady Catherine and blind prejudice by Mrs Bennet.

But we should guard against treating pride and prejudice as simple labels that we attach to characters and their behaviour. Jane Austen takes a far more complex view of human nature.

First, neither pride nor prejudice are fixed attributes of human beings, nor are they always distinguishable from other human characteristics. Tucked away in one of the novel's less significant corners, is an observation by the bookish Mary on the subject of pride: 'Vanity and pride are different things .... A person may be proud without being vain. Pride relates more to our opinion of ourselves, vanity to what others think of us' (Ch. 5, p. 20). As ever, Mary is ignored, but her declaration deserves examination:

● We may see that when Lady Catherine appeals to Elizabeth's sense of 'honour', 'decorum' and 'prudence' (Ch. 56, p. 286), she is not so much taking pride in her high moral standards as displaying her vanity by trying to protect her basest interests in a most aggressive and arrogant way.

● Similarly, Caroline Bingley's 'superciliousness' (Ch. 6, p. 2) and snobbery towards almost everybody, thinly disguised by her

CHECK THE BOOK

In a dictionary find as many meanings of 'pride' as you can and see how they may apply to *Pride and Prejudice*.

GLOSSARY
superciliousness
snootiness

outward charm, soon merges into jealousy towards Elizabeth. Her transparent attempts to ingratiate herself with Darcy reveal the true vulgarity that hides behind the proud public face.

- Mr Collins's inflated pride in his own true worth is easily seen as no more than vanity and conceit and even the amiable Sir William Lucas's understandable pride in his title is a gentle vanity.

- Lady Catherine, Caroline, Mr Collins and Sir William all exhibit the kind of pride that Mary identifies as vanity; essentially, they are most concerned with their public image.

- Charlotte is rather different: she displays no vanity but in agreeing to marry Mr Collins, Elizabeth feels she has disgraced herself. Charlotte lacks personal pride and shows a readiness to compromise her judgement in a way that Elizabeth would never entertain

There is another side to the question, however, which is concerned with how we judge others. *Pride and Prejudice* is based on an earlier novel, which has not survived, called *First Impressions*. The title is helpful because it alerts us to the dangers of making crude judgements about people without knowing enough about them. To do so is to invite prejudice:

- Elizabeth rushes to damn Darcy on insufficient evidence and she is also ready to judge him in the simplest possible terms.

- Darcy *is* proud but Elizabeth mistakes his proud manner for the kind of patronising arrogance displayed by his aunt.

- The way tenants are treated makes the difference clear: Darcy cares, Lady Catherine interferes.

Jane Austen goes even further to suggest that how well we know others is also dependent on how well we know ourselves:

- Elizabeth is predisposed to be won over by the rakish Wickham, because of her prejudices towards Darcy. When the truth emerges, she has to admit to herself how her powers of judgement had failed her (see Chapter 36).

 DID YOU KNOW?
During the eighteenth century, the French aristocracy began (rather too late for most!) to cultivate the concept of *noblesse oblige*, the notion that the nobility had responsibilities as well as rights and powers – Darcy has exactly this sense of duty, but (significantly?) he is not a nobleman.

- Darcy, too, reassesses his pride in both mind and deed. He sets his dignity aside to come to the aid of Lydia and Wickham and lays bare his mistaken understanding of himself to Elizabeth: 'I was given good principles, but left to follow them in pride and conceit' (Ch. 58, p. 297).

The conclusion we must draw is that 'rational' love is selfless and devoid of any vain pride and thoughtless prejudice, but to achieve that state one must first know oneself.

STRUCTURE

Jane Austen based her plot on the familiar format of the **romantic** novel:

- The heroine, who is lively and attractive but not glamorous, becomes acquainted with the hero who is in some way mysterious or even threatening.

- She is repulsed but he is captivated.

- Events and feelings force them apart but the reader knows they are really being drawn together.

- For a while, she is distracted by a false lover but when his wickedness is exposed, her eyes are opened to the hero's virtues.

- But it all seems too late; there are insuperable obstacles to their ever being united, until that is, the hero secretly takes decisive action and intervenes.

KEY EPISODES

There are a number of key episodes and events – the two balls, the extended visit to Netherfield, Wickham's revelations, Bingley's sudden return to London – leading up to Darcy's proposal that turns Elizabeth against him. His letter and the visit to Pemberley transform her feelings but Lydia's sudden elopement appears to snatch happiness from her grasp. Darcy's decisive intervention and Elizabeth's equally decisive defiance of Lady Catherine rescue her from the brink.

CHECK THE BOOK
Pick up almost any 'Mills and Boon' or similar publication to see how the romantic *conventions* still apply.

The structure, however, is not simply to do with Elizabeth and Darcy. The plot and the themes overlap and intertwine in a fascinating variety of ways. The main romance runs in parallel with the romance of Bingley and Jane. The marriage of Charlotte and Mr Collins both deepens our understanding of the theme of marriage and provides the vital narrative link with Lady Catherine.

Also important to the design of the novel are the two major changes of scene: the visits to Kent and Derbyshire. As well as creating interest for the reader through the introduction of new situations and characters, they offer new moral and emotional perspectives.

CHARACTERS

ELIZABETH

Elizabeth Bennet stands at the centre of the novel. She is the heroine but also the eyes through which we see and judge most of what happens. She is less beautiful than her elder sister, Jane, but has a natural vivacity and an endearing lack of stuffiness. She lacks Jane's reserve and **ironically** shares something of Lydia's wilfulness, if not her waywardness. She is the favourite of Mr Bennet and she inherits his sense of the ridiculous. For instance, Mr Collins's introductory letter leaves them both in amused amazement: 'Can he be a sensible man, sir?' (Ch. 13, p. 56).

Vivacious
Engaging
Strong-willed
Thoughtful
Witty
Caring
Perceptive

Mr Bennet recognises her 'quickness' (Ch. 1, p. 6) and Mr Darcy admires the 'liveliness' (Ch. 60, p. 306) of her mind. Certainly she relishes the cut and thrust of stimulating conversation and is always prepared to cross swords with the mighty Darcy. In Chapter 11, for instance, responding to one of Darcy's provocative remarks, Caroline titters 'How shall we punish him for such a speech?' (Ch. 11, p. 50). It is Elizabeth, however, who rises to the challenge. The reader, of course, knows that it is at such moments that Elizabeth is unconsciously drawn to Darcy. However much she may resent him, his proud, Olympian manner speaks of wider horizons and richer stimulus than Longbourn can offer. It is noticeable that she takes little part in the everyday chitchat of her mother and her younger sisters and she shows no interest in their regular visits to the local milliner's.

She is also a strong-minded person who will not compromise her principles and self-belief. She is reluctant to place marriage at the centre of her ambitions without any regard for feelings and circumstances. She is shocked by Charlotte's single-minded vision of marriage and she has no hesitation in rejecting two financially advantageous proposals.

Her strength of character is matched by her insight and sensitivity. For example, she is quick to see through the Bingley sisters' superficial civility and shares the pain that Jane must feel when she eventually accepts the truth about her false friend. In fact, her own feelings and attitudes are tightly bound up with concern for her elder sister. The first reason she offers for rejecting Darcy is that he had ruined 'perhaps for ever, the happiness of a most beloved sister' (Ch. 34, p. 158). Later, even though she is on tenterhooks concerning Darcy's feelings towards her, she is still deeply anxious for Jane's happiness and is delighted when she sees that Bingley must still love her.

For all her readiness to argue her corner and act in ways that Caroline Bingley, for instance, considers unladylike, her behaviour is always civilised, with a lack of affectation and pretence that is the sign of true good-breeding. As a consequence, her awareness of her family's deficiencies is acute. Her mother's and Lydia's ignorant vulgarity is a source of continuing shame but her sensitivity to Mr Bennet's weakness and lack of parental control is even more painful. Darcy's reflections on her family's 'total want of propriety' (Ch. 35, p. 163) only serve to confirm her perceptions.

At the same time, she is nothing less than a loyal and respectful daughter. She has the family's interests at heart when she tries to dissuade her father from allowing Lydia to go to Brighton but she accepts his misguided decision without further question. The affair of Lydia is especially wounding to Elizabeth: 'the mischief of neglect and mistaken indulgence towards such a girl. – Oh! how acutely did she feel it!' (Ch. 46, p. 227). Her shame is intensified by thoughts of what Darcy must think, and despair of him ever again having any regard for her. Even so, she is still able to feel sorry for her father and when Lady Catherine confronts her with the scandal, she is fiercely loyal. She takes the attack on her youngest sister as a personal insult and firmly dismisses her Ladyship.

CHECKPOINT 24

Why does Jane Austen present Elizabeth as being less beautiful than Jane, for example?

 CHECK THE BOOK

Look up 'propriety' in a dictionary. It means rather more than rudeness or lack of manners.

GLOSSARY

propriety 'correct' behaviour

For all her maturity and clear-sightedness Elizabeth does, of course, completely misjudge Darcy. The transformation of her 'prejudice' against him into 'pride' in his character and achievements, is the subject of the novel's central narrative thread. The painful process from dislike to admiration and love, reveals Elizabeth's ability to overcome her indignation and subject herself to ruthless self-examination. She does not simply *react* to Darcy's letter, she *analyses* it. All of which leaves open the question of how she could delude herself so comprehensively in the first instance. The simple answer is hurt pride stemming from Darcy's disparaging remarks at the first assembly. However, to nurture a grudge or to dwell on a passing remark is not in Elizabeth's character; she is even able to behave with tolerable good-humour towards Wickham after his unforgivable behaviour.

CHECKPOINT 25

Why dosen't Elizabeth reveal directly to Wickham that she knows the whole truth?

A more interesting answer is that Darcy's apparent disdain represents a challenge to her individuality. Wickham's easy charms and cheap flattery, offer a brief diversion but, from the outset, it is Darcy who engages her energies most profoundly. His proud manner sparks her defiance, which in turn engages his admiration. At the conclusion of the tale, Elizabeth herself analyses her attractions for Darcy:

> The fact is, that you were sick of civility, of deference, of officious attention. You were disgusted with women who were always speaking and looking, and thinking for *your* approbation alone. I roused, and interested you, because I was so unlike *them*
>
> (Ch. 60, p. 306)

Ultimately, it is her resilience and sense of humour that distinguishes Elizabeth and enables her to see her affairs in a sane and civilised perspective – 'I dearly love a laugh' (Ch. 11, p. 50). The one wifely task that she sets herself, is to nurture Darcy's underdeveloped sense of humour.

DARCY

Mr Darcy is immensely rich and powerful. He is a man of the world, who thinks nothing of travelling fifty miles in half a day, an unimaginable feat for most people of the time. In modern terms, he would be a leading member of the jet-set. Such people can easily arouse resentment and he is no exception: the people of Meryton soon mark him down as 'haughty', 'reserved' and 'the proudest, most disagreeable man in the world' (Ch. 3, p. 12). He is, however, well qualified as a romantic hero. There is an air of assurance about him and even a sense of danger in his cold manner. However, he attributes his reserve to his natural shyness, whilst his housekeeper maintains it is because he does not wish to show off like other young men. Nevertheless, he does not suffer fools gladly and by his own admission his 'good opinion, once lost is lost for ever' (Ch. 11, p. 51). There is, of course, much at Longbourn and Meryton to provoke his intolerance. Apart from the general narrowness of country life (Chapter 9), he has Mrs Bennet's embarrassing coarseness, Sir William's overfamiliarity, Mr Collins's lack of decorum and, although not directed at him, Lydia's impertinent reminder of Bingley's promise to mount a ball. More seriously, his concerns about the Bennet family's social inferiority cause him to 'detach' Bingley from Jane and outrage Elizabeth when first he proposes to her. He treats Mrs Bennet's rudeness with silent disdain and Mr Collins's uninvited attentions with 'distant civility' (Ch. 18, p. 83), but he also has a dry and economical **wit** that can readily dispose of those who should know better. For instance, Caroline Bingley's brainless attempts at flattery (Chapter 10) are dismissed with dead-pan politeness.

Aloof
Reserved
Assured
Shy
Decisive
Responsible

Public and private faces

As with all romantic heroes, there is a hidden side to Darcy, which is revealed when Elizabeth visits Pemberley. The other, positive aspect of his pride is a sense of duty to ensure the wellbeing of those in his charge. He is well-loved by his employees and tenants; the warmth of his love for his sister is plain to see and to Elizabeth's 'astonishment' (Ch. 43, p. 203) she learns that his housekeeper never had a cross word from him in her life.

However, his pride in his status and his pride in his sense of responsibility become confused in his treatment of Bingley. Eventually, he has to admit that his attempts to interfere in Bingley's life had been 'impertinent' (Ch. 58, p. 298). The key to the realisation that he had been 'selfish and overbearing' (Ch. 58, p. 297) is Elizabeth's accusation that he had not behaved in a gentleman-like manner. Through Elizabeth's prompting, he learns that while status is important, in the last analysis, true breeding is not dependent on rank.

GLOSSARY
officious intrusive
approbation approval
impertinent rude, inappropriate

JANE BENNET

Miss Bennet is the eldest of the sisters and the most handsome. She has a serene personality that always seeks to see the best in everybody. This generous outlook, in many ways so admirable, proves the source of her own distress. Her misplaced trust in Caroline Bingley leaves Jane exposed and unsuspecting of the true reasons for Bingley's absence. However, Jane proves wiser than Elizabeth when she feels certain that there must be more to the relationship between Wickham and Darcy than first appears.

Jane and Elizabeth

Handsome
Gentle
Generous
Vulnerable

Throughout the novel Jane and Elizabeth maintain a close and loving relationship. In fact, it sometimes seems as if Elizabeth is the elder sister, such is Jane's apparent innocence in the ways of the world. It is Charlotte that points out that Jane is too diffident and inclined to hide her feelings (Chapter 6). Elizabeth defends her sister at the time but later has to agree with Darcy about her sister's apparent indifference to Bingley. Jane is stoical about her disappointment in love but Elizabeth is able to see her true misery. Such is her lack of confidence, that to the near despair of Elizabeth, she refuses to recognise that Bingley's renewed attentions on his return are anything more than signs of casual friendship. The interrupted but gentle romance of Jane and Bingley, in which simple, unassuming virtue is rewarded, forms a charming contrast to the more tempestuous affair of Elizabeth and Darcy.

EXAMINER'S SECRET

Jane takes a back seat to Elizabeth in the novel and is easily ignored. But it's valuable to list examples of how Elizabeth's feelings and actions are influenced by consideration for Jane.

BINGLEY

Charles Bingley is the 'single man in possession of a good fortune' alluded to in the first sentence. In fact, it is not his wealth but his friendly, unaffected and unassuming character that impresses. Unlike his friend Darcy and his sister Caroline, he is devoid of snobbery. He is not a reflective person, preferring to act on the spur of the moment, but he is loyal. Before meeting him, Mrs Gardiner is somewhat sceptical about the reported violence of his passions, but, in fact, his devotion to Jane is unwavering. However, he is too easily influenced. Darcy's snobbery and his sisters' maliciousness force Bingley and Jane apart. **Ironically**, it is Darcy's 'conversion' that opens the way for their reunion.

Sociable
Affable
Warm-hearted
Impressionable

WICKHAM

Wickham is a version of the corrupt, pleasure-loving rake who is an essential ingredient of the eighteenth-century **romantic** novel, somewhat watered down to suit the lighter, comic tone of *Pride and Prejudice*.

Outwardly charming and plausible, he is an excellent conversationalist who engages everyone's sympathy for his supposed injustice at the hands of Darcy. The truth is that he is a cowardly spendthrift and a liar who is prepared to exploit women for personal pleasure and material gain. There is a hint of something particularly unsavoury about his attempted seduction of Georgiana and his elopement with Lydia, both of whom are attractive girls in their mid-teens. In both cases, it is Darcy who saves the young women from ruin.

Smooth-talking
Entertaining
Deceitful
Mercenary
Unprincipled

MRS BENNET

Mrs Bennet is possibly Jane Austen's best-known comic character. Her obsession with marrying off her five daughters results in all kinds of absurdities, comic subterfuges, knowing winks and violent mood swings between depression and ecstasy. She is the centre of numerous scenes of acute embarrassment, such as the occasion she loudly professes her dislike of Mr Darcy within his earshot (Chapter 18).

Within the context of an essentially light-hearted story, Mrs Bennet, like Mr Collins, may seem mere **caricature**, but we need shift our **point of view** only slightly to see her as a destructive influence. Her ignorant and superficial outlook leaves her devoid of any moral discrimination. Her hysteria at Lydia's elopement is outwardly comic but her concern for her daughter's wedding clothes in such dire circumstances is chilling.

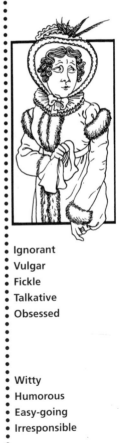

Ignorant
Vulgar
Fickle
Talkative
Obsessed

MR BENNET

Mr Bennet's easy **wit** and his wry sense of life's absurdities, not least his wife, are initially attractive; his remarks are always entertaining. However, it is especially painful to his favourite daughter, Elizabeth, that he has neglected his duties as a father. He is always ready to

Witty
Humorous
Easy-going
Irresponsible

DID YOU KNOW?

There is a play by Cedric Wallis called 'The Heiress of Rosings' (1956) which concerns, among other things, Mr Collins' affair with a chamber-maid! How convincing do you think that might be?

humour, mock or tease but never to intervene. Elizabeth largely blames him for Lydia's precocious and uncontrolled behaviour.

His attempts to track down Wickham and Lydia are hopelessly ineffective; he even neglects to write. On his return from London, he blames himself at first but his mock sternness towards Kitty is an early indication he cannot take his responsibilities seriously.

For a man of such sharp wit, he is curiously insensitive. His quip about Jane being able to enjoy the privilege of having being jilted is amusing but also rather cruel. He also displays a certain lack of principle. He is worried about how he is to repay his brother-in-law for supposedly securing a settlement with Wickham but such scruples vanish immediately he learns of Darcy's part in the affair. Furthermore, we learn at the last that he is quite content to trespass on Darcy's and Elizabeth's generosity by arriving at Pemberley unannounced.

MR COLLINS

Mr Collins is well summed up by Elizabeth: 'Mr Collins is a conceited, pompous, narrow-minded, silly man' (Ch. 24, p. 115). From his smug, self-regarding and impertinent introductory letter, his presence in the novel is virtually an endless illustration of Elizabeth's judgement. His servile praise of Lady Catherine seems inexhaustible, although he appears to make very little distinction between his patron and her possessions; he even knows how many windows grace the façade of Rosings.

Pompous
Absurd
Conceited
Fawning
Self-opinionated
Mercenary

His self-importance is comic because it reveals itself in extraordinary long-winded speeches and ponderous attempts at social grace. He is, however, a rather nasty character, who only escapes the charge of hypocrisy because of his complete lack of self-awareness. His superficiality is seen in the ease with which he is able to propose to both Elizabeth and Charlotte in the space of less than a week! For a clergyman, he possesses not a vestige of spirituality. Mr Bennet relishes his absurdity but Mr Collins's advice that the Bennet family should disown Lydia exposes his capacity for malice. As in the case of so many of Jane Austen's **caricatures**, the comic ridicule entertains but also cuts into the darker side of human nature.

LADY CATHERINE DE BOURGH

Lady Catherine's overbearing arrogance and sense of her own dignity is evident in all she says and does. Her sense of her unquestionable authority and right to control people's lives is most sharply seen when she confronts Elizabeth about her rumoured engagement to Darcy. Her enjoyment of flattery is no less sickening than Mr Collins's enthusiasm to give it; Elizabeth's preparedness to disagree with her is received with incomprehension.

Her tastes are vulgar and ostentatious and her professed love of music is a sham. In many ways she is a kind of aristocratic Mrs Bennet, sharing with Elizabeth's mother a brashness and rudeness that stems from a lack of innate intelligence and breeding. Her attitudes and behaviour offer an illuminating contrast to Darcy's.

**Snobbish,
Overbearing
Self-centered
Tactless**

LYDIA BENNET

Lydia is the youngest of the five daughters and is fifteen when the novel opens. She is described as 'well-grown' with 'high animal spirits' (Ch. 9, p. 40). Her smiling face and confidently provocative manner make her very attractive to men. She is totally selfish and her only thought is for her own pleasure: 'In Lydia's imagination, a visit to Brighton comprised every possibility of earthly happiness' (Ch. 41, p. 190).

She is unaware how vulnerable she really is and she is easy prey for one such as Wickham. However, she is not the least chastened by her adventure and treats it all as a huge joke. Least of all is she able to appreciate the distress she has caused her family. She does, of course, have the uncritical support of Mrs Bennet, whom she so closely resembles.

**Superficial
Irresponsible
Fun-seeking
Flighty**

CAROLINE BINGLEY

Miss Bingley's superficial civility thinly disguises her bitchiness. She is rich, regards herself a member of the social elite but lacks appropriate dignity and style. She treats Jane abominably and jealously tries to discredit Elizabeth in Darcy's eyes. However, her cheap jibes and

**Proud
Superficial
Undignified
Vindictive**

crude sarcasm serve only to emphasise her desperation and have a counterproductive effect on Darcy.

CHARLOTTE LUCAS

Honest
Supportive
Reliable
Unimaginative

Within the scheme of the novel, Charlotte is regarded as a kind of failure and disappointment. In settling for Mr Collins she appears to have compromised all sensible principles in the quest for security and comfort.

DID YOU KNOW?
Charlotte's life is dull but secure. Were she not married, one of the few options for her would have been to become a governess (or tutor) like Jane Eyre.

Importance in the novel

Elizabeth is shocked but Charlotte possesses neither Jane's beauty nor Elizabeth's confidence and wit. Her pragmatic approach to marriage may be restricted, but within the wider context of society at large, it probably represents a more realistic goal than that achieved by Elizabeth or Jane. Charlotte is a sensible woman who seems well able to adapt to her new circumstances. However much Elizabeth may take pity on her, Charlotte's chosen lot must be weighed against the fickle and unsettled lifestyle of Lydia and Wickham.

LANGUAGE AND STYLE

Jane Austen herself thought that *Pride and Prejudice* was 'rather too light and bright and sparkling'. Whether she was right or not, she is admired worldwide for her polished, precise style. Jane Austen never wastes words. As you read the novel you should pay careful attention to the implications and associations of the words she has chosen. She does not use a lot of metaphors and imagery, and description of settings are rare, but she is very skilled in choosing just the right word or phrase. For example, when Mrs Bennet learns that Lydia is married to Wickham, her spirits are 'oppressively high' (Ch. 50, p. 280); Lady Catherine enters the room with an air 'more than usually ungracious' (Ch. 56, p. 283), and for Mr Bennet, his cousin was 'as absurd as he had hoped' (Ch. 14, p. 59).

VOICES

Jane Austen's characters all speak in distinctive ways which reveal their attitudes and personalities. This adds to what we find out about them through their actions. For instance, Mr Bennet's dry wit is outwardly humorous but has a bitter edge to it that reflects the exasperation and tired resignation that years of marriage have produced:

> 'You mistake me, my dear. I have a high respect for your nerves. They are my old friends. I have heard you mention them with consideration these twenty years at least'   (Ch. 1, p. 6)

This in part shows why he has involved himself less in the upbringing of his daughters than, in retrospect, he should have done.

Mr Collins's pomposity is partly revealed by his being incapable of employing one word if six will do. He loves the sound of his own voice. The content of his speeches is almost always something to do with his own ideas or interests and their construction is long-winded, ponderous and in danger of losing its way:

> 'If I,' said Mr Collins, 'were so fortunate as to be able to sing, I should have great pleasure, I am sure, in obliging the company with an air; for I consider music as a very innocent diversion, and perfectly compatible with the profession of a clergyman'   (Ch. 18, p. 85)

Mrs Bennet's shallow, frivolous, overexcitable nature is reflected in this response to the news of Elizabeth's engagement to Darcy, where she speaks in endless exclamations and repetitions, with her focus still on material wealth and status, and her own 'nerves':

> 'I am so pleased – so happy! Such a charming man! – so handsome! so tall! – Oh, my dear Lizzy! pray apologise for my having disliked him so much before. I hope he will overlook it. Dear, dear Lizzy! A house in town! Everything that is charming! Three daughters married! Ten thousand a year! Oh lord! What will become of me. I shall go distracted'.   (Ch. 59, pp. 304–5)

There is also another important voice in the novel, that of Jane Austen herself. She tells the story as an omniscient narrator (one who knows about everything happening in the novel). At times she actually

EXAMINER'S SECRET
An 'A' student is able to provide a detailed account of language features, or structured patterns, to support a conclusion about the author's intentions.

GLOSSARY
distracted distraught; mad

comments in the first person on her characters: For example on Mrs Bennet,

> I wish I could say, for the sake of her family, that the accomplishment of her earnest desire in the establishment of so many of her children produced so happy an effect as to make her a sensible, aimiable, well-informed woman for the rest of her life...
>
> (Ch. 61, p. 310)

At other times you will need to read more carefully so see where the author is putting across her views:

> Miss Lucas, who accepted him solely from the pure and disinterested desire of an establishment, cared not how soon that establishment were gained.
>
> (Ch. 22, p. 103)

Even more of a challenge to the reader are those times when Jane Austen's voice blends in with that of one of her characters, as in this comment:

> Elizabeth saw directly that her father had not the smallest intention of yielding; but his answers were at the same time so vague and equivocal, that her mother, though often disheartened, had never yet despaired of succeeding at last.
>
> (Ch. 39. p. 183)

IRONY

There are times when as readers we must think very carefully whether the words Jane Austen uses can be taken at face value or whether she is creating humour or satire by being **ironic**. For example, at the end of the novel she records that Lady Catherine eventually decided to visit Pemberley, 'in spite of the *pollution* its woods had received ...' (Ch. 61, p. 312, italics added). (She sees Elizabeth as the source of the pollution.) The wishful thinking of Mrs Bennet is mocked by the irony of the statement, 'To be fond of dancing was a certain step towards falling in love' (Ch. 3, p. 11). Mr Bennet's irony is totally lost on Mr Collins; 'Risk any thing rather than her displeasure; and if you find it likely to be raised by your coming to us again ... stay quietly at home' (Ch. 22, p. 104). Elizabeth's critical attitude to Mr Darcy is veiled in this ironic response to Colonel Fitzwilliam; 'Oh! Yes, ... Mr Darcy is uncommonly kind to Mr. Bingley, and takes a prodigious deal of care of him' (Ch. 33, p. 153).

EXAMINER'S SECRET
Students who are alert to Jane Austen's sense of irony will impress. Mrs Bennet lacks a sense of irony and takes Mr Collins at face value; Elizabeth and her father see the man's absurdity.

DIALOGUE AND CONVERSATION

Talk is central to Jane Austen's novels. It ranges from passages of dialogue between intimates such as Jane and Elizabeth to set piece conversations like those between Elizabeth and Darcy at Netherfield, and the confrontation of Elizabeth and Lady Catherine. However, the novel is not a play script because, in addition to their words, we are presented with the characters' attitudes and reactions.

LETTERS

Some twenty-eight letters are referred to in the novel. It is believed that the earliest version of the story was in the form of an **epistolary** novel (one written entirely in letters). These letters help the story to progress by telling the characters (and the reader) about events they were not present at, summarise complicated series of events such as the search for Wickham and Lydia, and they remind us of the influence or role of characters who are not physically present. They also reveal a good deal about character by allowing us to 'hear' very different voices, for example of Darcy and Mr Collins. The letters also provide situations in which the recipient has time to reflect on events and the reader gains a unique insight into their feelings and reactions, such as Darcy's letter after his proposal to Elizabeth.

> **DID YOU KNOW?**
>
> In a way the letter is being re-invented in the form of e-mail and text messages – with a difference though!

CHARACTERS AND CARICATURES

Jane Austen 'grades' her characters, as it were. Elizabeth is the most complex and we view her in close-up. Darcy is presented in rather less detail, whilst Jane and Bingley are even more straightforward. Much of the novel's interest and fun lies in the way these 'normal' characters come in contact with the **caricatures**, notably Mrs Bennet, Mr Collins and Lady Catherine.

DETAILS

Pride and Prejudice is full of details that sum up a whole situation or character in a few words. Here are some examples:

- 'Mr Darcy said very little, and Mr Hurst nothing at all …. The latter was thinking only of his breakfast' (Ch. 7, p. 30)

- 'Lady Lucas, who had been long yawning at the repetition of delights which she saw no likelihood of sharing, was left to the comforts of cold ham and chicken' (Ch. 18, p. 84)

- 'In as short a time as Mr Collins's long speeches would allow, everything was settled' (Ch. 22, p. 102)

- 'Her home and her housekeeping, her parish and her poultry, and all their dependent concerns, had not yet lost their charms' (Ch. 38, p. 178)

DESIGN AND PLOTTING

Unlike later nineteenth-century novelists, notably Dickens, Jane Austen makes little, if any, use of description, **metaphor** or **symbolism** to convey character or theme. Instead, she relies on carefully selected and sequenced scenes and events to project developing feelings, attitudes and relationships, rather in the manner of a modern soap opera. In addition, the outward action is interwoven with the narrator's insight into the main character's inner thoughts and feelings.

EXAMINER'S SECRET
An A-grade candidate can analyse a variety of the writer's techniques.

Jane Austen owed much of her literary style, not only to novelists, but to the eighteenth-century tradition of essay writing. As a result each chapter is to a degree self-contained, with a distinct opening and conclusion. The novel's first sentence is justly famous but if you examine the opening of each chapter, you will see that a situation, time or place is firmly established:

Till Elizabeth entered the drawing-room at Netherfield …
(Ch. 18, p. 76)

More than once did Elizabeth in her ramble in the Park, unexpectedly meet Mr. Darcy …
(Ch. 33, p. 151)

It was the second week in May …
(Ch. 39, p. 180)

Two days after Mr. Bennet's return …
(Ch. 49, p. 243)

The chapter openings are very direct. The endings are often more reflective, offering a kind of summary or judgement on what has just taken place:

> Miss Bennet was the only creature who could suppose there might be any extenuating circumstances in the case, unknown to the society of Hertfordshire; her mild and steady candour always pleaded for allowances, and urged the possibility of mistakes – but by everybody else Mr. Darcy was condemned as the worst of men.
>
> (Ch. 24, p. 117)

A change of place, whether an enforced visit to Netherfield, a stay at Hunsford or a tour of Pemberley is invariably the signal for a major development in the plot, but it is also worth noting that Jane Austen is constantly changing scene in small ways in order to throw the focus on different characters or aspects of the theme. Chapters 1 and 2 take place in the Bennet home. Chapter 3 moves to the ball. In Chapter 4 Elizabeth and Jane are back home, but alone. In Chapter 5 the scene shifts to the Lucas home, and so on. In this respect Jane Austen anticipates the techniques of modern soap opera.

Another rather modern feature is the use of overlapping plot. As one plot-line is suspended, so another is introduced, typically in the form of a new character such as Wickham or Mr Collins. Of course, we eventually learn that the new plot-lines are closely linked with the first events.

Jane Austen also relies quite heavily on coincidence. How likely is it that Mr Bennet's estate should happen to be entailed to an obnoxious clergyman, whose living is in the gift of Lady Catherine, who just happens to be Darcy's Aunt?

For the most part, *Pride and Prejudice* deals in small events and is as remote from a Bruce Willis film as can be imagined, so the one really dramatic event, Lydia's elopement, is a pivotal moment in the plot's development. It occurs just at the point when Elizabeth and Darcy seem to be drifting into a comfortable resolution of their differences. Whilst creating a seemingly insurmountable obstacle, it actually provides the springboard for the novel's rapid progress to its conclusion.

EXAMINER'S SECRET

A candidate who is capable of arriving at unusual, well-supported judgements *independently* is likely to receive the highest marks.

Now take a break!

PART FOUR

HOW TO USE QUOTATIONS

One of the secrets of success in writing essays is the way you use quotations. There are five basic principles:

❶ Put inverted commas at the beginning and end of the quotation.

❷ Write the quotation exactly as it appears in the original.

❸ Do not use a quotation that repeats what you have just written.

❹ Use the quotation so that it fits into your sentence.

❺ Keep the quotation as short as possible.

 DID YOU KNOW?

These days, 'disinterested' is often confused with 'uninterested'. They do not mean the same thing.

Quotations should be used to develop the line of thought in your essays. Your comment should not duplicate what is in your quotation. For example:

> **Elizabeth thinks Jane is sweet, disinterested and angelic when she says 'Your sweetness and disinterestedness are really angelic' (Ch. 24, p. 114).**

Far more effective is to write:

> **When Elizabeth tells Jane 'Your sweetness and disinterestedness are really angelic' (Ch. 24, p. 114) she shows her concern that Jane is too good-natured and reticent.**

However, the most sophisticated way of using the writer's words is to embed them into your sentence:

> **The 'wild giddiness' (Ch. 37, p. 175) of Kitty and Lydia was just one example of the 'the folly and indecorum' (Ch. 37, p. 175) of her family which made Elizabeth feel so ashamed.**

When you use quotations in this way, you are demonstrating the ability to use text as evidence to support your ideas – not simply including words from the original to prove you have read it.

COURSEWORK ESSAY

Set aside an hour or so at the start of your work to plan what you have to do.

- List all the points you feel are needed to cover the task. Collect page references of information and quotations that will support what you have to say. A helpful tool is the highlighter pen: this saves painstaking copying and enables you to target precisely what you want to use.

- Focus on what you consider to be the main points of the essay. Try to sum up your argument in a single sentence, which could be the closing sentence of your essay. Depending on the essay title, it could be a statement about a character: Although Charlotte's willingness to settle for the safety of 'a comfortable home' shocks Elizabeth, it was a wholly understandable decision for a twenty-seven-year-old woman with an uncertain future; an opinion about setting: The elegance of Pemberley's grounds reflects the good taste of its owner; or a judgement on a theme: In *Pride and Prejudice* Jane Austen demonstrates that happiness and harmony are achieved only if we are prepared to see ourselves, as well as others, with fresh eyes.

- Make a short essay plan. Use the first paragraph to introduce the argument you wish to make. In the following paragraphs develop this argument with details, examples and other possible points of view. Sum up your argument in the last paragraph. Check you have answered the question.

- Write the essay, remembering all the time the central point you are making.

- On completion, go back over what you have written to eliminate careless errors and improve expression. Read it aloud to yourself, or, if you are feeling more confident, to a relative or friend.

If you can, try to type your essay, using a word processor. This will allow you to correct and improve your writing without spoiling its appearance.

EXAMINER'S SECRET

Examiners have a pretty shrewd idea if you have copied from a book such as this or the internet. Don't! or you will lose marks.

GLOSSARY
folly foolishness
indecorum 'improper' behaviour

EXAMINER'S SECRET
A feature of 'A'-grade writing on literature is the ability to see two possibilities of interpretations and to support a preference for one of them.

SITTING THE EXAMINATION

Examination papers are carefully designed to give you the opportunity to do your best. Follow these handy hints for exam success:

BEFORE YOU START

- Make sure you know the subject of the examination so that you are properly prepared and equipped.

- You need to be comfortable and free from distractions. Inform the invigilator if anything is off-putting, e.g. a shaky desk.

- Read the instructions, or rubric, on the front of the examination paper. You should know by now what you have to do but check to reassure yourself.

- Observe the time allocation – and follow it carefully. If they recommend 60 minutes for Question 1 and 30 minutes for Question 2, it is because Question 1 carries twice as many marks.

- Consider the mark allocation. You should write a longer response for 4 marks than for 2 marks.

WRITING YOUR RESPONSES

- Use the questions to structure your response, e.g. question: 'The endings of X's poems are always particularly significant. Explain their importance with reference to two poems.' The first part of your answer will describe the ending of the first poem; the second part will look at the ending of the second poem; the third part will be an explanation of the significance of the two endings.

- Write a brief draft outline of your response.

- A typical 30-minute examination essay is probably between 400 and 600 words in length.

- Keep your writing legible and easy to read, using paragraphs to show the structure of your answers.

- Spend a couple of minutes afterwards quickly checking for obvious errors.

WHEN YOU HAVE FINISHED

- Don't be downhearted – if you found the examination difficult, it is probably because you really worked at the questions. Let's face it, they are not meant to be easy!

- Don't pay too much attention to what your friends have to say about the paper. Everyone's experience is different and no two people ever give the same answers.

EXAMINER'S SECRET
The examiners have read the novel, so they don't need to be told the story. Refer to aspects of the plot – do not write it out in detail.

IMPROVE YOUR GRADE

KNOW YOUR TEXT

Whatever text you are studying, it is vital that you are really familiar with its contents. These Notes are intended to help you find your way around *Pride and Prejudice* but they are **not** a substitute for reading the novel itself.

There are two essential aspects of the novel you need to master:

- THE PLOT: make sure you know the order of events and who does what at various stages in the story.

- THE CHARACTERS: make sure you know who's who, what they do and say.

Knowing the plot and the characters leads to the most **basic** understanding of the text. You need to know these things **before** you can begin to answer any question.

You need to test yourself in some way to make sure you really do know what happens and who the characters are. Break the novel down into sections. Make simple notes on the key events. Don't just rely on guides such as this or your teacher's notes but make your own diagrams or flow charts so that you can find your way around the novel in the way suits **you** best.

You could, for instance, divide the novel into five main sections, Chapters 1-12, 13-23, 24-38, 39-50, 51-61, that correspond to the divisions of the **General summary** in this guide and make your own plan of each on five separate sheets of paper.

You could also concentrate on particular episodes, such Jane's stay at Netherfield or Elizabeth's visit to Hunsford.

Remember it is easier to learn in small doses than commit everything to memory at once.

EXAMINER'S SECRET

Long quotations are not very effective. *Pinpoint* the key words – do not rely on them 'being in there somewhere'.

KEEP A QUOTATION BOOK

Select the key quotations (you will find many in this guide, printed in purple) and put them into a little notebook. You will find that by listing quotations in this way you get to know them far more easily than if you have to rummage around a 300 page novel every time.

You could also link each quotation with what it illustrates. For instance: 'Lady Catherine listened to half a song, and then talked' (Ch. 31, p. 144) – shows Lady C's rudeness and lack of culture.

A quotation book works the other way about too: it provides you with a set of examples to back up your comments.

Remember, even if you are able to take your text into the examination, if you don't know what quotations you want to use, you can waste a lot of time searching for them.

THINK ABOUT THEMES AND CHARACTER

Although you must obviously know the plot, if you want to gain a good grade examiners want to know if you can do more than retell the story. This means you must be prepared to do some *interpretation* of the text.

You might start with the title: **Why is the novel called** *Pride and Prejudice?*

● You should ask yourself about the possible meanings of the words in the title.

- When is pride a good quality and when is pride a bad thing? What examples can you point to in the story?

- There are, in fact, over 50 direct uses of the words 'pride', 'proud' or 'proudly' in the novel, as well as all those occasions where pride is shown but the word itself is not used.

- The first instance is in Chapter 3; Darcy is referred to as 'the proudest, most disagreeable man in the world' (p. 12). Contrast that opinion with Elizabeth's self-reproach as she acknowledges that Darcy's proposals 'which she had proudly spurned only four months ago, would now have been gladly and gratefully received!' (Ch. 50, p. 252), and you start to build up a picture of all the different points of view and 'prejudices' which the story reveals.

EXAMINER'S SECRET

Pride and Prejudice is a long, detailed novel. It is impossible to master it all at once. It is better to build up some solid thoughts about the main characters and ideas, than try to remember everything.

Remember ideas intertwine and the work you do in following up one theme can almost certainly be directed at another. The two lines just quoted may help us to think about the idea of pride but they also get us thinking about Elizabeth and Darcy.

You should also think about **how** Jane Austen creates her world. This can be a very complicated issue and many students find it very difficult to write about authors' methods. The section on **Language and style** may help you get started.

Try, as far as possible, to gather some solid examples that you **really understand.** For instance, you could look at how Jane Austen builds up a picture of that giddy teenager, Lydia, partly through direct comment, partly through her reported actions and partly through the way she speaks. Look at her letter (Ch. 47). Compare it to some of the other letters in the novel. Would any other character have begun with the words, 'You will laugh when you know where I am gone' (p. 236)?

BEFORE THE EXAMINATION
Getting your ideas straight

Too often students find themselves with huge folders of assorted notes, guides, videos, etc. not to mention the novel itself. **You cannot possibly memorise or use the lot!** In an examination you are required to write a short essay, perhaps not much more than 600 words. So it is a good idea to reduce all that baggage to something you can handle.

Try producing a single revision sheet for each of the key characters and themes. Set it out in the form of a diagram with essential quotations and some phrases **of your own**.

THE EXAMINATION!

EXAMINER'S SECRET

Keep the precise words of the question in front of you during the examination. Check at regular intervals that you are still answering the question. A surprising number of candidates drift off the subject after a good start.

Read the question

Ask any examiner what lets down candidates the most and the answer will be **failure to read the question**.

The danger is that often candidates want to write **all** they know about a subject when the question asks them to focus on a particular aspect. So there is no point in including a long account of Mr Collins's proposal if the question asks about his life with Charlotte in Kent.

Look carefully at the **exact** words of the question especially if it has more than one part. Take for example the question: '**Describe the life of Mr Collins and Charlotte in Hunsford and why it dismays Elizabeth**'.

The first part of the question asks you to provide specific **information** while the second half of the question looks for **comment**.

Take your time – keep your wits about you

Don't begin writing until you have worked out more or less what you want to say otherwise you may end up writing quite the wrong thing. Plan your answer.

As you write, check that you are still answering the question. It is surprisingly easy to start well and drift off the subject entirely.

Watch the clock

It's important to distribute your time effectively. If you have two questions to answer in two hours, it really is advisable to spend about an hour on each even if you know more about one topic than another. Any marks gained by a lot of extra time spent on one question is unlikely to make up for marks lost on another.

What the examiners are looking for

Examiners are looking for evidence of knowledge and understanding but the evidence can take many forms, some more effective than others.

Lets consider possible treatment of the question 'How effective is the opening chapter of *Pride and Prejudice?*'

Basic

The key word in this question is *effective* but the weakest candidates will concentrate on the **literal** information, make very simple statements and probably use fairly simple vocabulary in their account. They may begin along these lines:

> The opening chapter of *Pride and Prejudice* is very effective when it says a 'single man in possession of a good fortune, must be in want of a wife' (Ch. 1, p. 5).
>
> Mrs Bennet says that a man has moved into Netherfield. She says he is single also that she wants her daughters to marry.
>
> Mr Bennet laughs at Mrs Bennet who gets quite mad. She was a bit stupid.
>
> Jane Austen makes it very funny.

That would be a very simple answer. It shows some knowledge of the text; there is a direct quotation, two characters are correctly identified and the nature of the conversation is at least recognisable. At the same time, the first sentence simply echoes the question and says nothing about **why** it is effective. Similarly, the scene is certainly 'funny' but no reason or support is given. It's quite true that Mrs Bennet is 'stupid' but it is a very crude term that doesn't tell us much about the character.

Candidates at this level would gain some credit for the information they provide but they would need to provide more comment, preferably with examples, to gain more marks.

EXAMINER'S SECRET
Simply writing what happens will gain you only a few marks.

Better

At the next level candidates will pay some attention to the specific question, start to make some connected comments **with support from the text** and write with more sensitivity.

They may begin along these lines:

> The first sentence refers to a single man needing a wife which tells us that the novel is going to be about marriage. This is confirmed when Mrs Bennet makes clear that she wants one of her daughters to marry the rich young man who has just moved into Netherfield: 'You must know that I am thinking of his marrying one of them' (Ch. 1, p. 5).
>
> We learn that Mrs Bennet is obsessed about seeing her daughters married because, while Mr Bennet appears to show no interest in visiting the new neighbour, she becomes more and more agitated. We see this when she says, 'Mr. Bennet, how can you abuse your own children in such a way? You take delight in vexing me. You have no compassion for my poor nerves' (Ch. 1, p. 6).
>
> The scene also tells us something about the Bennet family and how Mrs Bennet's narrow-minded outlook contrasts with her husband's 'sarcastic humour' (Ch. 1, p. 7).

EXAMINER'S SECRET
The best candidates are able to *cross-reference* by showing the connections between different parts of the text.

First of all, this opening displays some consideration of how the first chapter is effective. It suggests that the opening conversation picks up the theme of marriage which was planted in the first sentence. There is also comment on Mrs Bennet's character based on the **evidence of the text**. Her mood is also more closely defined; she is not 'mad' this time but 'agitated'.

The last sentence tells us something of the **specific** information that the first chapter introduces.

Best

The best candidates do not necessarily see any need to tell the story – they know the examiner has read the book. They concentrate on **comment** and the **author's** methods and achievement.

They may begin along these lines:

> We are plunged into the world of marriage and manners from the opening sentence of the novel which proclaims that a rich young man 'must be in want of a wife' (Ch. 1, p. 5). At first this strikes us as absurd but the conversation between Mr and Mrs Bennet demonstrates that for some it really is a 'truth universally acknowledged' (Ch. 1, p. 5) as is shown by the fact that the business of Mrs Bennet's life 'was to get her daughters married' (Ch. 1, p. 7).
>
> Mr and Mrs Bennet come alive in the first chapter through their conversation. We see how Mrs Bennet's moods can swing from joy at the prospect of one of her daughters marrying the newcomer, to exasperation and sulkiness the next moment. We may also laugh at Mr Bennet's witty teasing of his wife and her predictable responses, although we learn later his 'sarcastic humour' (Ch. 1, p. 7) leans towards irresponsibility.

This response attempts to **integrate** comment, account and reference. Quotations such as 'truth universally acknowledged' are used as part of the argument rather than simply tagged on to a comment.

Notice how there is no attempt slavishly to work through the chapter. The quotation concerning Mrs Bennet's business in life is drawn from the chapter's last sentence.

Some brief thought is given to how the Mr Bennet's behaviour anticipates later developments.

By the use of such terms as 'joy', 'exasperation' and 'sulkiness', there is an attempt to define Mrs Bennet' reactions as precisely as possible.

EXAMINER'S SECRET
You should use a *range* of words to describe characters and different aspects of their personalities.

SAMPLE ESSAY PLAN

A typical essay question on *Pride and Prejudice* is followed by a sample essay plan in note form. This does not present the only answer to the question, merely one answer. Do not be afraid to include your own ideas and leave out some of the ones in this sample! Remember that quotations are essential to prove and illustrate the points you make.

What part does Lady Catherine play in *Pride and Prejudice*?

PART 1   INTRODUCTION

Lady Catherine's role may be considered from three points of view:

- Her character and what it represents

- How she relates to other characters

- Her part in the development of the story

EXAMINER'S SECRET

You should try to show how different aspects of character interact by using words such as 'however', 'on the other hand' or simply 'but' – 'Lady Catherine is proud but vulgar'.

PART 2   CHARACTER

She represents undisguised pride at its most arrogant.

We initially learn of her from Mr Collins and she is first presented in the scenes at Rosings. Mr Collins's servility in itself suggests a woman who is excessively vain and self-important and this is confirmed in the way in which she soaks up compliments and dominates the conversation.

She has the inbred sense of superiority that is associated with her position in society. She is an old-world aristocrat who thinks she has the right to interfere in other people's lives such as those of her tenants and other local people and then later, Elizabeth's. This behaviour contrasts with Darcy's responsible sense of duty towards his tenants and employees.

Her vain pride is also reflected in her vulgarity and lack of taste, represented in the contrast between Pemberley with Rosings – her £800 fireplace is a sign of ostentatious wealth. Her professed love for music is a sham.

Her insolence towards Elizabeth shows lack of true breeding and shows her to be no more refined than Mrs Bennet at the other end of the social scale.

PART 3 RELATIONSHIPS

She brings out the best in Elizabeth first at Rosings and then later at Longbourn. Her arrogant pride which amounts to insolence contrasts with Elizabeth's integrity. We also see by *contrasting* the two characters that Elizabeth has superior intelligence and manners. At Rosings Darcy is embarrassed for Elizabeth by Lady Catherine's rudeness, just as Elizabeth had been embarrassed by her mother.

PART 4 NARRATIVE ROLE

She is the catalyst that finally brings Elizabeth and Darcy together, first by confronting Elizabeth then by reporting the interview to Darcy.

EXAMINER'S SECRET
Plan your answers then you won't repeat yourself.

FURTHER QUESTIONS

Make a plan as shown above and attempt these questions.

❶ What different aspects of marriage are presented in *Pride and Prejudice*?

❷ Explain why Darcy's proposal is a turning point in the novel.

❸ Why does her visit to Pemberley make such an impression on Elizabeth.

❹ Give an account of Elizabeth's relationships with her family.

❺ In what ways does Elizabeth show an independent mind?

❻ What are Darcy's virtues?

❼ How does Jane Austen show that Mrs Bennet is 'a woman of mean understanding, little information, and uncertain temper'?

❽ What are Mr Bennet's strengths and weaknesses?

❾ How does Jane Austen demonstrate that Mr Collins is 'a conceited, pompous, narrow-minded, silly man'?

❿ In what ways is Wickham important to the plot and themes of *Pride and Prejudice*?

anticlimax an often humorous effect created by the sudden descent.from the important or high sounding to the trivial or banal. The effect is expressed in the phrase 'from the sublime to the ridiculous'

caricature [note the spelling] the presentation of character through the exaggeration of particular personality features, often used to ridicule failings such as vanity and pomposity

convention common, recognizable features within a particular art-form such as the 'shoot-out' in a Western, or the visit to the cellar in a horror film. Jane Austen uses the 'conventions' and familiar features of the romantic novel to her own ends.

denouement the final unfolding of the plot enabling it to move towards its proper conclusion

epistolary written in the form of letters

irony (adj. ironic) basically saying one thing but meaning another, it can take many forms. An episode in the plot may be ironic because it has a significance not evident at the time or an expression may be ironic because it suggests other meanings than the literal sense

metaphor a metaphor is when two different things or ideas are fused together: one thing is described as being like another

omniscient (narrator) the assumption that the storyteller has knowledge of everything including what the characters are thinking

parody a conscious imitation of a style for comic effect

point of view a complex aspect of narrative that concerns whose thoughts or attitudes are being represented. They may be those of the character, the narrator, the author or the reader

Romantic(ism) a term relating to the artistic movement that began towards the end of the eighteenth century and stressed the importance of emotion and individual imagination

romantic fiction (romance) a popular form of sentimental love story

satire writing which exposes the follies of human behaviour by presenting it as absurd or ridiculous

symbolism something simple which represents something else more complicated (often an idea or quality) e.g. a flag symbolising national identity

wit a blend of humour, intelligence and verbal brilliance

CHECKPOINT HINTS/ANSWERS

CHECKPOINT 1 The opening sentence is constructed so as to create an **anticlimax**. The phrase 'a truth universally acknowledged' (Ch. 1, p. 5) sounds as if it is going to lead on to a matter of great seriousness but the idea that the 'truth' is that any rich young man is 'in want of a wife' seems preposterous. We are all above that sort of thing, aren't we? At the same time, as we discover, young women, the Bennet sisters in particular, *needed* to marry for the sake of their own security. The question is how much does love play a part in the equation.

CHECKPOINT 2 Charlotte seeks security above all else (and hence marries Mr Collins quickly even though she does not love him); Elizabeth thinks love must play its part (and eventually marries Darcy after she is convinced they both truly love each other). Neither is entirely right or entirely wrong.

CHECKPOINT 3 Entailment was a legal device to avoid estates being broken up by ensuring inheritance passed through a male line. In the absence of an immediate male relative, the estate could pass through entailment to a 'distant relation' (Ch. 7, p. 27) such as Mr Collins who might be a total stranger to the family. Mrs Bennet is all too aware that because the estate is entailed, her daughters must marry if they are to retain their status.

CHECKPOINT 4 The Bingley sisters are relieved at the imminent departure of Jane and Elizabeth.

CHECKPOINT 5 The Bennet sisters are the daughters of a gentleman and cooking was not an appropriate pursuit for gentlewomen.

CHECKPOINT 6 Although he is a clergyman ready to lecture others about their moral conduct, Mr Collins's fondness for gaming reveals his underlying worldliness.

CHECKPOINT 7 Elizabeth's readiness to believe Wickham is fuelled by her dislike of Darcy.

CHECKPOINT 8 Jane's strength is not to rush to judgement in the way that Elizabeth is quick to support Wickham and condemn Darcy. Her weakness is she is too trusting and is later badly hurt by Caroline Bingley, for instance.

CHECKPOINT 9 Mrs Bennet is a woman of 'uncertain temper' (Ch. 1, p. 7) and her moods are always extreme, so Charlotte's engagement is a bitter blow and 'Nothing could console' (Ch. 23, p. 107).

CHECKPOINT 10 Although Elizabeth is not exactly jilted by Wickham, Mr Bennet's remark is more prophetic than he can imagine.

CHECKPOINT 11 It confirms Elizabeth's prejudice towards him, that he is proud and disagreeable.

CHECKPOINT 12 Elizabeth's glee at seeing that Miss de Bourgh, supposedly promised in marriage to Mr Darcy, is so sickly demonstrates that Darcy is never far from her mind.

CHECKPOINT 13 The early visit to Hunsford is a sign of Darcy's eagerness to see Elizabeth; he cannot possibly want to see Mr Collins.

CHECKPOINT 14 Both Darcy and Elizabeth respond in similar ways to Lady Catherine's manner, although nothing is said at this point.

CHECKPOINT 15 Mr Darcy is stung by Elizabeth's suggestion that he had not behaved in a 'gentleman-like manner' (Ch. 34, p. 159). Pride in being a true gentleman is at the core of Darcy's character.

CHECKPOINT 16 Elizabeth remembers how Charlotte had warned that Jane should be more positive in showing her attachment to Bingley.

CHECKPOINT 17 If Mr Bennet had known the truth about Wickham he might have refused to allow Lydia to go to Brighton.

CHECKPOINT 18 Lydia too marries for superficial reasons.

CHECKPOINT 19 Lydia's letter reveals her as flighty and thoughtless. She does not think to write to her family, everything is treated as a joke and there is no thought that anyone should be worried.

CHECKPOINT 20 Mrs Bennet is ignorant of the truth and hints pointedly that Darcy has let Wickham down.

CHECKPOINT 21 Although Elizabeth laughs at herself when she looks forward to 'another Mr. Collins' (Ch. 55, p. 282), there is a sense that if she had more of Charlotte's determination, she would not be facing an insecure future.

CHECKPOINT 22 Despite her personal misgivings about the behaviour of her family, Elizabeth will not tolerate them being insulted by the arrogant Lady Catherine. She is after all, 'a gentleman's daughter' (Ch. 56, p. 287).

CHECKPOINT 23 It's ironic that Mrs Bennet, who was so eager for Elizabeth to marry Mr Collins, should question her desire to marry Darcy, the biggest catch of all.

CHECKPOINT 24 To emphasise that it is her wit and personality that attracts Darcy.

CHECKPOINT 25 Perhaps to tease him, perhaps not to seem triumphant or simply to act in a civilised way and not descend to Wickham's level.

TEST YOURSELF (CHAPTERS 1–12)

1 Mr Bennet *(Chapter 1)*

2 Sir William Lucas *(Chapter 5)*

3 Mary Bennet *(Chapter 6)*

4 Charlotte Lucas *(Chapter 5)*

5 Charles Bingley *(Chapter 3)*

TEST YOURSELF (CHAPTERS 13–23)

1 Elizabeth Bennet *(Chapter 16)*

2 Mrs Bennet *(Chapter 18)*

3 Mr Collins *(Chapter 18*

4 Mr Collins *(Chapter 13)*

5 Miss de Bourgh *(Chapter 14)*

6 George Wickham *(Chapter 15)*

TEST YOURSELF (CHAPTERS 24–38)

1 Jane *(Chapter 24)*

2 Mr Gardiner *(Chapter 25)*

3 Miss de Bourgh *(Chapter 28)*

4 Darcy *(Chapter 31)*

5 Darcy and Jane *(Chapter 33)*

6 Catherine (Kitty) and Lydia *(Chapter 37)*

TEST YOURSELF (CHAPTERS 39–50)

1 Darcy's housekeeper (Mrs Reynolds) of Wickham *(Chapter 43)*

2 Caroline Bingley of Elizabeth *(Chapter 45)*

3 Jane of her father *(Chapter 47)*

4 Mr Collins of Lydia's elopement *(Chapter 48)*

5 Mrs Bennet on hearing the news of the marriage settlement *(Chapter 49)*

TEST YOURSELF (CHAPTERS 51–61)

1 Lydia to Jane *(Chapter 51)*

2 Elizabeth to Lydia *(Chapter 51)*

3 Elizabeth to Jane *(Chapter 54)*

4 Lady Catherine de Bourgh *(Chapter 56)*

5 Mr Bennet *(Chapter 57)*

6 Darcy *(Chapter 58)*

NOTES

Maya Angelou
I Know Why the Caged Bird Sings

Jane Austen
Pride and Prejudice

Alan Ayckbourn
Absent Friends

Elizabeth Barrett Browning
Selected Poems

Robert Bolt
A Man for All Seasons

Harold Brighouse
Hobson's Choice

Charlotte Brontë
Jane Eyre

Emily Brontë
Wuthering Heights

Shelagh Delaney
A Taste of Honey

Charles Dickens
David Copperfield
Great Expectations
Hard Times
Oliver Twist

Roddy Doyle
Paddy Clarke Ha Ha Ha

George Eliot
Silas Marner
The Mill on the Floss

Anne Frank
The Diary of a Young Girl

William Golding
Lord of the Flies

Oliver Goldsmith
She Stoops to Conquer

Willis Hall
The Long and the Short and the Tall

Thomas Hardy
Far from the Madding Crowd

The Mayor of Casterbridge
Tess of the d'Urbervilles
The Withered Arm and other Wessex Tales

L.P. Hartley
The Go-Between

Seamus Heaney
Selected Poems

Susan Hill
I'm the King of the Castle

Barry Hines
A Kestrel for a Knave

Louise Lawrence
Children of the Dust

Harper Lee
To Kill a Mockingbird

Laurie Lee
Cider with Rosie

Arthur Miller
The Crucible
A View from the Bridge

Robert O'Brien
Z for Zachariah

Frank O'Connor
My Oedipus Complex and Other Stories

George Orwell
Animal Farm

J.B. Priestley
An Inspector Calls
When We Are Married

Willy Russell
Educating Rita
Our Day Out

J.D. Salinger
The Catcher in the Rye

William Shakespeare
Henry IV Part I
Henry V
Julius Caesar

Macbeth
The Merchant of Venice
A Midsummer Night's Dream
Much Ado About Nothing
Romeo and Juliet
The Tempest
Twelfth Night

George Bernard Shaw
Pygmalion

Mary Shelley
Frankenstein

R.C. Sherriff
Journey's End

Rukshana Smith
Salt on the snow

John Steinbeck
Of Mice and Men

Robert Louis Stevenson
Dr Jekyll and Mr Hyde

Jonathan Swift
Gulliver's Travels

Robert Swindells
Daz 4 Zoe

Mildred D. Taylor
Roll of Thunder, Hear My Cry

Mark Twain
Huckleberry Finn

James Watson
Talking in Whispers

Edith Wharton
Ethan Frome

William Wordsworth
Selected Poems

A Choice of Poets

Mystery Stories of the Nineteenth Century including The Signalman

Nineteenth Century Short Stories

Poetry of the First World War

Six Women Poets

Margaret Atwood
Cat's Eye
The Handmaid's Tale

Jane Austen
Emma
Mansfield Park
Persuasion
Pride and Prejudice
Sense and Sensibility

Alan Bennett
Talking Heads

William Blake
*Songs of Innocence and of
Experience*

Charlotte Brontë
Jane Eyre
Villette

Emily Brontë
Wuthering Heights

Angela Carter
Nights at the Circus

Geoffrey Chaucer
The Franklin's Prologue and Tale
The Miller's Prologue and Tale
*The Prologue to the Canterbury
Tales*
*The Wife of Bath's Prologue and
Tale*

Samuel Coleridge
Selected Poems

Joseph Conrad
Heart of Darkness

Daniel Defoe
Moll Flanders

Charles Dickens
Bleak House
Great Expectations
Hard Times

Emily Dickinson
Selected Poems

John Donne
Selected Poems

Carol Ann Duffy
Selected Poems

George Eliot
Middlemarch
The Mill on the Floss

T.S. Eliot
Selected Poems
The Waste Land

F. Scott Fitzgerald
The Great Gatsby

E.M. Forster
A Passage to India

Brian Friel
Translations

Thomas Hardy
Jude the Obscure
The Mayor of Casterbridge
The Return of the Native
Selected Poems
Tess of the d'Urbervilles

Seamus Heaney
*Selected Poems from 'Opened
Ground'*

Nathaniel Hawthorne
The Scarlet Letter

Homer
The Iliad
The Odyssey

Aldous Huxley
Brave New World

Kazuo Ishiguro
The Remains of the Day

Ben Jonson
The Alchemist

James Joyce
Dubliners

John Keats
Selected Poems

Christopher Marlowe
Doctor Faustus
Edward II

Arthur Miller
Death of a Salesman

John Milton
Paradise Lost Books I & II

Toni Morrison
Beloved

George Orwell
Nineteen Eighty-Four

Sylvia Plath
Selected Poems

Alexander Pope
*Rape of the Lock & Selected
Poems*

William Shakespeare
Antony and Cleopatra
As You Like It
Hamlet
Henry IV Part I
King Lear
Macbeth
Measure for Measure
The Merchant of Venice
A Midsummer Night's Dream
Much Ado About Nothing
Othello
Richard II
Richard III
Romeo and Juliet
The Taming of the Shrew
The Tempest
Twelfth Night
The Winter's Tale

George Bernard Shaw
Saint Joan

Mary Shelley
Frankenstein

Jonathan Swift
*Gulliver's Travels and A Modest
Proposal*

Alfred Tennyson
Selected Poems

Virgil
The Aeneid

Alice Walker
The Color Purple

Oscar Wilde
The Importance of Being Earnest

Tennessee Williams
A Streetcar Named Desire

Jeanette Winterson
Oranges Are Not the Only Fruit

John Webster
The Duchess of Malfi

Virginia Woolf
To the Lighthouse

W.B. Yeats
Selected Poems

Metaphysical Poets